The
Church
at
Worship

GAINES S. DOBBINS

What can ministers do to increase the meaning and value of worship and acquire a measure of proficiency in the conduct of worship? Where can they gain insights and skills for leading others in worship? No person is better qualified to offer guidance in this most important area than Dr. Dobbins, who has taught a course in worship through most of his long career as a seminary professor.

This book is a basic study of the purpose of public worship and what worship should mean to growing Christians. It offers principles rather than precepts and specific plans. Such topics as Recovering the Original Pattern, Confronting the Hindrances, Examining Ways of Worship, Planning and Conducting the Worship Service, Magnifying Music in Worship, Enriching and Expanding Worship, Linking Evangelism with Worship, and Evaluating Worship are skilfully developed in clear, readable style.

(Continued on back flap)

The Church at Worship

The
Church
at
Worship

. . .

GAINES S. DOBBINS

1083

BROADMAN PRESS
Nashville, Tennessee

BV
15
.D6

422-172

Library of Congress catalog card number: 63:7334
Printed in the United States of America
5.MY6213

*To the multitude of former students
who have shared with me in the quest for
a more effective leadership of worship*

Preface

Always worship has been a major concern of the churches of every order. Worship practices have varied from extreme formalism to extreme informality, but some activity intended to give expression to God-consciousness is an invariable aspect of all church services. Yet the importance and true nature of these performances are not always clearly perceived. In this book the effort is made to recover the primacy of worship and to clarify its meaning and purposes.

In many religious circles there is deep concern for the improvement and enrichment of worship. Churches that have long followed a prescribed order are re-examining their liturgies with a view to a larger measure of spontaneity and vitality. Churches that have gloried in their freedom from form are recognizing the value and even necessity of more carefully structured and enriched services of worship. As these extremes move toward the center, they find themselves approaching the New Testament pattern and meeting more satisfyingly human need today.

This book is intended to serve a fourfold purpose: (1) to magnify the importance and confront the difficulties of worship today; (2) to clarify the meaning and objectives of contemporary worship; (3) to propose ways of conducting and enriching worship; (4) to link worship with Christian education and evangelism. My long teaching experience in this field leads me to believe that there is a felt need for such a volume, both as a text and for general use.

Appreciation is due publishers who have granted privilege to use copyrighted materials which, of necessity, I have quoted freely. To my colleagues of the faculties of Southern Seminary and Golden Gate Seminary I am grateful for encouragement which they have given. To my wife I give thanks for her patience and yet her urgency that I complete this manuscript as one above others in which she has been especially interested.

GAINES S. DOBBINS

Contents

1

Worship, the Sustaining Motive for Churchgoing

There was a time when churchgoing on the part of self-respecting citizens of a typical American community was taken for granted. Indeed, if we go back to colonial days, church attendance in one New England state was legally compulsory. Even when there was no legal requirement, churchgoing was almost a necessity, since on Sunday there was seldom anywhere else to go. For many years so-called "blue laws" closed places of entertainment or amusement on Sunday, giving to the churches a practical monopoly of Sunday assemblage.

Nothing in American life has more radically changed than Sunday observance and church attendance. For many, Sunday is just another work day. For many more, who do not work, Sunday is a holiday, not a holy day. The invasion of the home by the Sunday newspaper, radio, and television has further secularized what was once the day of worship. Although churchgoing is maintained at relatively high levels in American communities, it is being more and more seriously threatened. While Sunday morning services may still be well attended, Sunday evening services are becoming increasingly difficult to maintain, and the midweek "prayer meeting" is ignored by the majority of church members.

Intelligent Christians know that "going to church" is not the whole of Christian living, and ministers realize that maintaining attendance at stated services is not the measure of his or the church's success. But members and ministers must recognize that empty pews are a church's chief liability and constitute warning signals of impending failure for the total church enterprise.

Attracting, holding, and serving religious congregations is serious "big business," the success or failure of which may not be taken lightly. On a typical weekend in the United States more than a quarter-million ministers will conduct religious services in places of worship attended by approximately one fourth the population. Countless hours will go into the preparation of these services. Thousands of songs will be sung and millions of words spoken in the course of the activities. A vast amount of time will be consumed by pastors and people.

Why do these people go to church? Is it worthwhile? What difference does it make in their lives and in the life of the community? If churchgoing is of sufficient value to justify the presence of those who attend, why do many others neglect or refuse to go? What is the future of churchgoing? If it can be increased, what will be the outcome? If it declines, what will be the consequences?

Not opposition but sophistication threatens church attendance in today's culture. A sophisticate is one who has lost the sense of wonder. Modern sophistication is the product of urbanization and is closely associated with a cynical and materialistic view of life. It becomes fashionable for many to speak of God, religion, and the church as outmoded and Christian standards of conduct as old-fashioned. To the city sophisticate, churchgoing may be just a gesture of respect to the past, or the way to pass an occasional hour, or left to country cousins, or even opposed as retarding progress. To the rural sophisticate, churchgoing takes time and money from the struggle to wrest a precarious profit from a reluctant soil. To many city and country dwellers alike, to go to church would seem "the most wasted hour of the week."

Will sophistication eventually eliminate worship or will the human dilemma call even the worldly-wise back to the place where God is recognized and his will sought? Have the churches something to offer so universally needed that even sophisticates will attend their services in search of ultimates? May we not assume that underneath the veneer of superiority is deep-felt need that is not being met by the world? This spiritual hunger is for God and can be satisfied only by the experience of worship.

Sophisticated men without God have in this tragic twentieth century already brought to the world unparalleled destruction. Sophisticated men without God now threaten civilization with total destruction. Churchgoing is a matter, therefore, of far greater moment than filling churches and supporting religious institutions—it is vital to the peace of the world and the welfare of mankind. No matter how ministers may rationalize, congregations apologize, and cynics criticize, when church attendance falls off in a community or a nation, the threat of ruin grows more imminent.

Such considerations call for a re-examination of men's motives in attending or not attending church. If the reasons for attending are superficial or unworthy, churchgoing will quite likely become sporadic or cease altogether under pressure of other interests and demands. Ministers and churches are seriously risking decline who take for granted that unexamined and inadequate motives for church attendance will continue indefinitely to bring even their own members to the church services. Even more important is the necessity for inquiry into the motives of those who do not attend.

Why do many people neglect or refuse to go to church? Obviously, not because beautiful and comfortable buildings are lacking, nor because of lack of elaborate and ornate rituals, nor because of lack of trained and competent leaders of worship. Often attendance is poorest where these provisions are most adequate. Sometimes attendance is most gratifying where buildings and ceremonials and trained leaders are conspicuously absent. We need to search deeper for reasons for nonattendance.

Survey interviews have disclosed a variety of replies to the inquiry, "Why do you or do you not go to church?"*

Positively, such answers as these are typical:

"I feel better when I go."
"I like the music."
"I love God and want to be with his people."
"I want to learn to be more like Jesus."

---

*From survey reports of students in the author's classes in worship, Golden Gate Baptist Theological Seminary, Mill Valley, California.

4

THE CHURCH AT WORSHIP

"The Bible teaches me to go."
"Going to church is my witness for Christ."
"I go to learn what the Bible says."
"I like to listen to the sermon."
"I go from a sense of duty."
"I enjoy the fellowship of friends who attend."
"I gain spiritual strength for the week ahead."
"I see more clearly the true values of life."
"My sins are rebuked and forgiven and my ideals restored."
"God becomes more real and Christ draws nearer."
"Worship clarifies my thinking and helps me solve my problems."
"I feel that something is missing if I do not go."
"I want to share in winning the lost to Christ."

Negatively, these replies were typical:

"Going to church depresses me—I feel uncomfortable."
"I was compelled to go as a child—it was punishment!"
"Churchgoers impress me as too smug and complacent."
"My job requires that I work on Sunday."
"My parents were not churchgoers—I never got the habit."
"Going to church is not necessary to be a Christian—I can worship just as well at home."
"I don't believe in God—I can't worship a nonexistent being."
"Too many churchgoers are hypocrites."
"Churches are religious rackets—all they are after is the money."
"Churches are outworn and useless institutions."
"The church is on the wrong side—it's for management, not labor."
"Communism is right—religion is an opiate of the people."
"Church people are insincere and self-righteous."
"I can get all the church offers elsewhere."
"Most sermons are dull and boring."
"Churchgoing doesn't make much difference in the way people live."
"Sunday is my only day off—I need it for other things."
"I am too preoccupied with other things—churchgoing does not appeal to me as being important."

Is it not noteworthy that some of the reasons for going to church are about as unconvincing and superficial as the reasons for nonattendance? Responses would of course vary from community to community, but there is reason to suspect that the inquiry would sum up to much the same conclusion: the motives of churchgoers and nonchurchgoers need re-examination.

The roving reporter for the *San Francisco Chronicle* stopped several persons on the busy streets of the city and asked: "Why do people go to church?" Here are some of their replies:

"I was brought up in a Christian family, but attending college changed my views. I learned that church is not the biggest part of Sunday living. It's more important when you grow older, though, because of fear of death."

"Obviously, there is no God; so people who go to church are following blindly the folkways and attitudes of society. Their parents told them to eat peas with a fork and go to church, but people should think for themselves."

"I go to church because I believe what my church has to say, but most people go because they think it's the thing to do and they enjoy dressing up on Sunday morning. I'd say the type that goes is the average American."

"It's a crutch. People derive a certain amount of pleasure from church. It makes them happy, and everybody is after happiness. But on top of that, these people are genuinely intrigued with the idea."

"People feel a need for whatever church gives them, like a chance to relax and think in peace. The environment has a lot to do with it. Stained glass and the building are conducive to thought. That's the setting and that's why we have churches."

"I don't think they go for very much spiritual guidance. They like the minister to say what they want him to say, but they don't really want to live the Ten Commandments. They don't really practice what is being preached."

"It gives people a feeling of security. Some are sincere and others go as a sort of social outlet. But it makes you feel better, and afterward the soul rests easier for the following week of sin."

"People feel closer to God when they are in a house of worship. It gives them peace of mind, and my parents always said church was relaxing. But if there is a God, I don't think you need to go to church to pray to him."[1]

It is interesting to note that only one of the persons interviewed (a student) gave as the primary reason for church attendance that "people feel closer to God when they are in a house of worship." Even he seemed to be somewhat skeptical about the existence of

God and did not think that it was necessary to go to church to pray. Evidently those who go to church and those who do not too often have in common the motive of self-interest. The churchgoers appear to be saying that they attend because of what they get out of it; the nonchurchgoers say that they stay away because attendance doesn't pay.

Is there not a deeper motive for churchgoing which should appeal to the two groups alike? The answer, simple in statement but profound in application, is: people go to church to worship God. The distinctive purpose of churchgoing is to experience the divine presence in the company of fellowseekers after God. True, God is not confined to a building made with hands but the building called a church is specifically the Lord's (*kuriakos*). The baptized believers who constitute "the body of Christ" are the church (*ekklēsia*), but this "gathered community" needs a meeting place. Worshipers meet together but they meet with the Lord. They come together claiming his promise to be in their midst. This is the master motive that sustains churchgoing.

Reasons for not going to church sum up to one of two things: there is no felt need or desire for going with others into God's presence; or going to church does not meet this need. If the sense of need of God is repressed or denied continuously, the soul atrophies and life becomes empty and hard. If the church does not satisfy this soul hunger for God, it becomes cold and empty.

Efforts to promote and maintain church attendance often indicate both the deep concern and the futile approaches to the solution of the problem. Attempts may be made to attract and hold audiences by means of sensational sermons, special entertainment and musical features, persistent and attention-compelling publicity, go-to-church campaigns, contests, appeals to loyalty of church organizations, warm and friendly welcome, appeals to duty, fear of consequence of nonattendance, incentives of reward—even to the offering of trading stamps and door prizes!

In the long run, such motives as these prove disappointing for sustained churchgoing. The sensational preacher loses his popularity, special features cannot long compete with commercial entertainment, campaigns and contests run aground, church organizations may slacken in loyalty, fellowship may be broken, fear of consequences is spiritually unhealthy, habit and duty may develop conflicts, rewards and prizes are contrary to the Christian spirit of self-sacrifice.

Empty pews are the most expensive item in the church budget. No matter how carefully lessons and programs and sermons are prepared, they are of little consequence to absentees. Music might as well have been confined to choir rehearsal if on Sunday only a handful of people are present to participate and appreciate. The financial support of the church and its worldwide causes will be beggarly if only a few are present to give when the collection plates are passed. Saddest of all, if only a few go to church, few or none will be won to Christ.

A church bulletin announced: "Due to power failure, there will be no worship tonight." The reference was to a break in the electric power line which deprived the church of light and heat and the use of the organ. The announcement might have been phrased: "Due to worship failure, there will be no power in the church." Worship has always provided the power by means of which God's people have carried out his purposes.

This principle of power through worship is clearly stated in Paul's prayer for the Ephesians, as he besought God on their behalf that he would give them a spirit of wisdom and revelation that they might come to know

what is the immeasurable greatness of his power . . . far above all rule and authority and power and dominion, and above every name that is named, not only in this age but also in that which is to come; and he has put all things under his feet and has made him the head over all things for the church, which is his body, the fulness of him who fills all in all (Eph. 1:19-23).

Are we not here at the heart of the answer to the question, "Who goes to church—and why?" Ultimately, people go to church and keep on going because there they come into confrontation with God in Jesus Christ and discover the meaning of life and find the power

needed for Christian living. When the centrality of God in Christ
is restored, when the power of the Holy Spirit is manifest through
the proclamation of the Scriptures and the testimony of the saved,
there will be given "power to comprehend with all the saints what
is the breadth and length and height and depth, and to know the
love of Christ which surpasses knowledge, that you may be filled
with all the fulness of God" (Eph. 3:18-19).

When a church leads people to an experience of worship that
enables them to approximate this ideal, it will have gone a long way
toward the solution of the problem of churchgoing.

2

Recovering the Original Pattern

Christian worship has its roots in ancient soil. An understanding of the worship of the churches today requires the exercise of historical memory. Indeed, worship antedates history. The archaeologist's spade has unearthed evidence of the universality of worship before there were written records of human activity. Christian worship has its distinctives, but it owes much to antecedent beliefs and practices.

The Genesis account of beginnings tells of communion between God and the man and the woman whom he made in his image. The account relates how sin separated man from his God, with resultant depravity. With Abraham began the recovery of monotheism. A new era in worship was introduced through Abraham's descendants, but worship did not originate with the Hebrews.

Primitive worship was intertwined with magic. In magic, control of supernatural power is sought through sacrifices, incantations, ceremonials; in worship, the worshiper submits himself to the control of divine power. Superstition is not readily distinguished from religious faith. Superstitious worship accords veneration to objects or persons in the belief that they can bring about effects without credible cause, as in witchcraft, apparitions, omens, charms. Intelligent religious faith is exercised when men put their trust in a purposeful divine being who can on occasion perform miracles but who customarily achieves his ends through the use of natural means. Even Christian worship may cling to some vestigial remainders of magic. The Old Testament records reflect a progressive development from a measure of superstition mixed with monotheistic faith to pure worship purged of idolatry.

Jacob worshiped God but he attributed the fact that his flocks

9

brought forth lambs that were "striped, speckled, and spotted" to their exposure to rods that were peeled with white streaks (Gen. 30:37-43). Jacob's family worshiped God but Leah thought that eating mandrakes enabled her to conceive and bear a son. When Jacob left Haran to return home with his family and possessions, Rachel stole her father's household gods and hid them in the camel's saddle upon which she sat, evidently looking to them for protection (Gen. 31).

Calf worship was common in Egypt and was not abandoned by the Israelites after their deliverance. While Moses was on Mount Sinai, receiving the tables of the law, the impatient people prevailed on Aaron to make a golden calf, which they worshiped with heathen revelry, attributing to it their deliverance from Egypt (Ex. 32:1-7).

Years later, Jeroboam, first king of the ten tribes following the division of the kingdom, made two calves of gold, repeating Aaron's words, "Behold your gods, O Israel, who brought you up out of the land of Egypt!" and sacrifices were offered to them at Bethel and Dan (1 Kings 1:25-33). Ahaz, king of Judah, burned his son as an offering and "sacrificed and burned incense on the high places" (2 Kings 16:1-4). Later, the blight of idolatry spread until it infected all Judah, resulting in widespread calf-worship, star-worship, Baalism, human sacrifice, divination, and sorcery (2 Kings 17:7-18). The subsequent disasters of destruction and exile are attributed to these evils of false worship.

Not only did the people of Israel substitute the magic of heathen gods for faith in Jehovah; even when they worshiped Jehovah, they brought to their worship concepts and practices that corrupted it. By means of elaborate ceremonials they undertook to gain God's favor or to put him under obligation to insure divine benefits. This lip service, in which form and ceremony took the place of heartfelt devotion and holy living, was as repugnant to God as idolatry. Isaiah thundered against this perversion of worship. He thus spoke for God:

> When you come to appear before me,
>   who requires of you
>   this trampling of my courts?

> Bring no more vain offerings;
>   incense is an abomination to me.
> New moon and sabbath and the
>   calling of assemblies—
>   I cannot endure iniquity and
>   solemn assembly.
> Your new moons and your appointed feasts
>   my soul hates;
> they have become a burden to me,
>   I am weary of bearing them (1:12-14).

Jehovah then declared the conditions necessary for true worship:

> When you spread forth your hands,
>   I will hide my eyes from you;
> even though you make many prayers,
>   I will not listen;
>   your hands are full of blood.
> Wash yourselves; make yourselves clean;
>   remove the evil of your doings
>   from before my eyes;
>   cease to do evil,
>   learn to do good;
>   seek justice,
>   correct oppression;
>   defend the fatherless,
>   plead for the widow (1:15-17).

In the light of this denunciation of ceremonialism, the question may be raised as to why so much is made of ceremonial and ritual in the Old Testament. Why were such elaborate details given for the construction of the Temple and why was so much emphasis placed on the forms to be used by the priests and their associates? Two reasons may be suggested: first, formless worship becomes empty and meaningless; second, careful prescription of worship was needed to safeguard it from the idolatry with which Israel was surrounded. Although the Israelites were God's chosen people, they were very human and needed to be guarded against confusing worship with magic and superstition.

The Babylonian Exile purged Israel of idolatry. The pendulum then swung to the other extreme. Worship became rigid, exacting. The sabbath became central in worship, and about it were gathered scores of burdensome rules and regulations. The Temple and the synagogue became exclusive places of worship, apart from which God was not to be found. Thus, the conviction became established that God could be worshiped by circumcised Jews only, in a place of worship belonging to them and with ceremonials of their devising. The interbiblical period, between Malachi and Matthew, represents four hundred years of this spiritual sterility.

Into this spiritual barrenness came Jesus Christ with his dynamic and revolutionary teaching, preaching, and practice. He attacked the lifeless formalism of Jewish worship and opposed the heavy burdens of the ceremonial law. He deliberately repudiated the cherished traditions of the rabbis concerning the sabbath and outraged them and their adherents by violating technical rules which they sought to enforce in order to obey the Third Commandment. He deliberately healed on the sabbath and declared that he, the Son of man, was Lord of the sabbath.

Indignantly he drove from the Temple the money-changers and those who made a racket of selling sacrificial animals at exorbitant prices, saying, "Is it not written, 'My house shall be called a house of prayer for all the nations'? But you have made it a den of robbers" (Mark 11:17). Scathingly he denounced the Pharisees for their hypocritical worship, pointing out that the heavy burdens they bound on others they themselves refused to bear. "They do all their deeds to be seen by men," he declared, "for they make their phylacteries broad and their fringes long, and they love the place of honor at feasts and the best seats in the synagogues, and salutations in the market places, and being called rabbi by men" (Matt. 23:5-7). To the Samaritan woman, who would have involved Jesus in an argument over the right place to worship, Jesus said, "neither on this mountain nor in Jerusalem will you worship the Father . . . . But the hour is coming, and now is, when the true worshipers will worship the Father in spirit and truth, for such the Father seeks to worship him. God is spirit, and those who worship him must worship in spirit and truth" (John 4:21-24).

Yet we are told that when Jesus returned to Nazareth, his native village, "he went to the synagogue, as his custom was, on the sabbath day" (Luke 4:16). Frequently it is reported that he taught and preached and healed in the synagogues. The only glimpse given of him in his youth is that of his visit to Jerusalem at the age of twelve. Here he was found "in the temple, sitting among the teachers, listening to them and asking them questions." To his mother's anxious inquiry, he replied, "How is it that you sought me? Did you not know that I must be in my Father's house?" (Luke 2:41-49). Jesus exposed the hollowness of ceremonial worship that lacked sincerity and reality, but he exalted true worship and respected the day and the house of worship.

Jesus was not the first to denounce formalism. To the disobedient Saul, Samuel said:

Has the Lord as great delight in
    burnt offerings and sacrifices,
  as in obeying the voice of the Lord?
Behold, to obey is better than sacrifice,
  and to hearken than the fat of rams.
For rebellion is as the sin of divination,
  and stubbornness is as iniquity and idolatry.
Because you have rejected the word of the Lord,
  he has also rejected you from being king
                    (1 Sam. 15:22-23).

The penitent David wrote:

    For thou hast no delight in sacrifice;
      were I to give a burnt offering,
        thou wouldst not be pleased.
    The sacrifice acceptable to God is
      a broken spirit;
    a broken and contrite heart, O God,
      thou wilt not despise (Psalm 51:16-17).

Isaiah declared with the voice of God:

      What to me is the multitude of your sacrifices?
      says the Lord;

> I have had enough of burnt offerings of rams
>   and the fat of fed beasts;
> I do not delight in the blood of bulls,
>   or of lambs, or of he-goats (Isa. 1:11).

Amos likewise spoke for God to declare: "I hate, I despise your feasts, and I take no delight in your solemn assemblies" (Amos 5:21).

Micah pleadingly questioned:

> With what shall I come before the Lord,
>   and bow myself before God on high?
> Shall I come before him with burnt offerings,
>   with calves a year old?
> Will the Lord be pleased with thousands of rams,
>   with ten thousands of rivers of oil?
> Shall I give my first-born for my transgression,
>   the fruit of my body for the sin of my soul?
>   (Mic. 6:6-7).

Notwithstanding this repudiation of formalism, John the Forerunner of Jesus used the ceremony of baptism in his public commitment of disciples to the coming one and as evidence of their repentance. Jesus swept away the elaborate rituals of Judaism but retained baptism and instituted the rite of the Lord's Supper. He invested both of these ceremonies with rich spiritual content. Baptism would symbolize his death, burial, and resurrection; and the death, burial, and resurrection with him of the believer. The Supper would symbolize his shed blood and broken body, the atoning sacrifice for sin, in partaking of which the baptized believer would refresh his memory concerning the price paid for his salvation and renew his sense of union with the Saviour. It is clear that baptism and the Supper were intended to be high and holy ceremonials of worship.

The early Christians continued for a time to attend the Temple and synagogue services. Later, the rift between Judaism and Christianity widened until it became evident that they could have no part with each other. Soon Christians as baptized believers formed a close fellowship, the *ekklēsia*, the church. Such a church was a separate visible community with simple organization for definite purposes. The writer of the letter to the Hebrews warned against "neglecting to meet together, as is the habit of some" (10:25). The book of Acts tells of Christian assemblies and Paul's letters throw light on them. The meetings were for several purposes. Meetings were held to express and deepen the sense of *koinōnia*—community—as when the Jerusalem Christians "devoted themselves to the apostles' teaching and fellowship, to the breaking of bread and the prayers" (2:42). There are some evidences of ritual, but the meetings for edification were informal and democratic, with almost unlimited freedom in worship.

The meetings for thanksgiving were apparently closely related to the observance of the Lord's Supper, the designation of which came to be "the Eucharist" (from *eucharistia,* thanksgiving). The observance of the Supper was often accompanied by a love feast *(agapē),* abuses of which were severely condemned by Paul (1 Cor. 11:17-22).

The democratic nature of the church found expression in the congregational business meeting, when affairs of the church were discussed and decisions made, when disputes among the brethren were settled, when disciplinary action was taken concerning false teachers or those guilty of unchristian conduct. Disorderly behavior in worship had developed. Paul dealt with the problem in his first letter to the Corinthians (chap. 14).

Observance of baptism and the Lord's Supper early became a point of departure from the simplicity of worship and life as indicated in the New Testament writings. Especially was there confusion concerning the Supper. Apparently there were those who identified it with the *kiddush,* a Jewish religious ceremonial meal eaten by the family in preparation for the observance of the sabbath. Others thought of it as a repetition of the Passover meal. In either case, the meal symbolized the fellowship of a household of faith united in bonds of loyalty. The "love feast" may have been eaten as the Memorial Supper, or the ceremony of the Supper may have followed the common meal. Such practices lent themselves to the perversions

of which Paul wrote when he told the Corinthians that it is not the
Lord's Supper that they eat when "each one goes ahead with his
own meal, and one is hungry and another is drunk" (1 Cor. 11:21).
An overemphasis on the social feature likewise led to the conception
of the Supper as a "communion" not so much with Christ as with
one another.

From the records, it is manifest that Jesus intended the Supper
to be a simple act of corporate worship. Jesus knew how easy it
would be for the disciples and those who succeeded them to forget.
With sublime simplicity, as Luke records the event, Jesus "took
bread, and when he had given thanks, he brake it, and gave to them,
saying, This is my body which is given for you: this do in remembrance of me. And the cup in like manner after supper, saying, This
cup is the new covenant in my blood, *even* that which is poured
out for you" (Luke 22:19-20, ASV). Paul adds that Jesus, following the eating of the bread, gave to the disciples the cup saying,
"This cup is the new covenant in my blood: this do, as often as
ye drink it, in remembrance of me. For as often as ye eat this
bread, and drink the cup, ye proclaim the Lord's death till he
come" (1 Cor. 11:25-26, ASV).

Undoubtedly the ceremonial was given as a memorial that reminded of Jesus' atoning death, that assured his promised presence,
and pointed to his coming again. Clearly, partaking of the bread
and wine would be meaningless to those who were not baptized followers. Perfectly it complements the ceremony of baptism, symbolizing the continuance of the Christian life just as baptism symbolizes its beginning. The two simple ceremonials would replace all
the elaborate ritualism of the Old Testament era. However, there
is no hint that Jesus attributed saving power to either of the ceremonies. Without doubt he intended that they should be perpetuated
and that they should be entrusted to his church for their administration. The early churches interpreted the mind of Christ when they
gave a central place to baptism and the observance of the Supper
as acts of worship. That he so ordained the observance has led many
Christians to prefer "ordinance" to "sacrament," since the latter
word came to be associated with the doctrine of substantiation, de-

noting the magical transformation of bread and wine into the literal body and blood of Christ and so possessing saving grace.

Many influences combined to change baptism and the supper from symbolic ceremonies to saving sacraments. Gradually the church was made a saving institution rather than an institution of the saved. Ministers became priests with sacerdotal powers. Baptism and the Supper were viewed as "mysteries," by means of which saving grace was mediated through the church by its priests. By Old Testament analogy, baptism replaced circumcision and the Supper replaced the Passover. In Roman thought, baptism and the Supper were equated with the *sacramentum*, the oath of allegiance that the officer or soldier took when initiated into the service of the emperor. Eventually baptism, administered usually in infancy, was endued with saving power; the observance of the Supper (or *mass*) became necessary to the sustaining of the life implanted through baptism. Gathered about the two original "sacraments" were five others—confirmation, penance, extreme unction, holy orders, and matrimony (the two latter being mutually exclusive). In the course of time elaborate rituals were devised for use on a variety of occasions denoted on the calendar of the church.

The two developments appear to have taken place simultaneously—the elaboration of worship and the corruption of doctrine. It would be difficult to say which was cause and which was effect. Generally, a practice is instituted and supporting doctrine is then formulated. If the Roman Church had maintained the pure worship of the first century, it would probably have been saved from the doctrinal perversions of the later centuries. It is, therefore, highly important to re-examine Christian worship if we are to account for the power of these early churches. We should then observe how spiritual power was lost as a concomitant of perverted worship and doctrine.

First-century Christians claimed the real presence and power of the living Christ. They revered the Old Testament Scriptures and used devoutly first the oral traditions and then the written records of the words and deeds of Jesus, but they lived and spoke in the conscious realization that he himself was with them. To Jesus Christ they gave supreme allegiance. They claimed no credit for their witness and its amazing results.

When Peter was haled to court by the Jewish rulers and asked, "By what power or by what name did you do this?" (Acts 4:7), referring to the healing of the lame man at the gate of the Temple, he boldly replied, "Be it known to you all, and to all the people of Israel, that by the name of Jesus Christ of Nazareth, whom you crucified, whom God raised from the dead, by him this man is standing before you well" (vv. 10-12).

In the letter to the Hebrews, Jesus Christ is exalted as the supreme object of worship to whom were applied the words of the psalmist, "Let all God's angels worship him," and "Thy throne, O God, is for ever and ever, the righteous scepter is the scepter of thy kingdom" (Heb. 1:6,8). The power of the witness and worship of these first Christians came from the realized presence of the living Lord.

The worship of the apostolic churches was characterized by radiance and joy. In Christ these Christians had found fulness of life. They were not saved from hardship, trial, persecution, or even death. But they were emancipated from slavery to things and freed from anxiety over earthly outcomes. Jesus had taught that blessedness would be the mark of the citizen of his kingdom. He had told them to "rejoice and be glad" even when persecuted. On the way to the cross he had said to the disciples, "I will see you again and your hearts will rejoice, and no one will take your joy from you. . . . In the world you have tribulation; but be of good cheer, I have overcome the world" (John 16:22, 33).

That the apostles took Jesus seriously was evidenced on the occasions when they were imprisoned and beaten because they continued to bear witness to Jesus. After the apostles had been beaten and charged not to speak in the name of Jesus, "they left the presence of the council, rejoicing that they were counted worthy to suffer dishonor for the name. And every day in the temple and at home they did not cease teaching and preaching Jesus as the Christ" (Acts 5:41-42). The letter to the Hebrews reflects the heart of early Christian worship: "I will proclaim thy name to my brethren, in the midst of the congregation I will praise thee" (2:12), referring to Jesus Christ. A church that has thus found the meaning of life in Christ and is joyfully sharing him with others is a church with power and cannot be defeated.

First-century Christians assembled in order to keep in touch with reality. Life had to be lived, often under hard circumstances. The Christian witness had to be borne in spite of temptations to evasion and compromise. Christian service to others had to be rendered notwithstanding their own need. Dissensions and heresies within the church had to be dealt with, even though it would have been easier to ignore the problems and difficulties. Worship had to be kept restrained and understandable without chilling the ardor of those whose enthusiasm led them to ecstatic "speaking with tongues." Baptism and the Lord's Supper had to be guarded lest these two simple rites became perverted into saving acts. Salvation by God's grace in Christ through repentance and faith alone had to be maintained in the face of the contention of the Judaizers.

When the church assembled, it was not just to listen to a sermon and join in songs of praise—the coming together of the baptized believers was for serious business in which all members had both the privilege and the responsibility to participate. Such participation was of the essence of worship. Divine guidance was sought and found that the life of the church might be made relevant to the affairs of men.

First-century Christians met for edification. It was recognized that Christians need to be "built up." Jesus said, "I will build my church," and in doing so he "went about all the cities and villages, teaching in their synagogues and preaching the gospel of the kingdom, and healing every disease and every infirmity" (Matt. 9:35).

How are Christians edified? According to the practice of Jesus, by engaging in teaching, preaching, and healing. Following Jesus' example, Christians are to "go about" carrying on this threefold activity. In order to teach, they must be taught; in order to preach, they must listen to preaching; in order to heal, they must themselves be healed. Are we not here at the heart of the purpose of churchgoing? A church with power is one made up of members who come together in the spirit of worship to be so taught and inspired that they will go out to share with others what they have received.

First-century Christians loved others. They realized they could not truly love God and not love people. They took Jesus at his word: "This is my commandment, that you love one another as I have loved you" (John 15:12). This love, they understood, must begin with "the household of faith." John proposed this evidence of salvation: "We know that we have passed out of death into life, because we love the brethren. He who does not love remains in death. Anyone who hates his brother is a murderer, and you know that no murderer has eternal life abiding in him." (1 John 3: 14-15). Bluntly John declared: "If anyone says 'I love God,' and hates his brother, he is a liar; for he who does not love his brother whom he has seen, cannot love God whom he has not seen. And this commandment we have from him, that he who loves God should love his brother also" (1 John 4:20-21).

Love like this is not an automatic endowment that comes with salvation. How is such love developed? In large measure it comes through the practice of corporate worship. When we worship together we forget our antipathies, we lose our prejudices, we become more tolerant of weaknesses, we forgive those who have trespassed against us. In worship we forget ourselves and see the needs of others. In worship we go toward that perfection which Jesus said belongs to God, who "makes his sun rise on the evil and on the good, and sends rain on the just and on the unjust" (Matt. 5:45). In worship we obey the injunction of Jesus: "Whenever you stand praying, forgive, if you have anything against any one; so that your Father also who is in heaven may forgive you your trespasses" (Mark 11:25).

When we turn from this intriguing picture of first-century Christians thus worshiping, and consider what transpires as worship in many churches today, are we not convinced that the twentieth century may well learn from the first?

3

Confronting Hindrances to Worship

Two faults contribute to the weakness of our worship services today—formalism and formlessness.

The early Christians, following the example and teaching of Jesus, went to the opposite extreme of Jewish formalism. This informality contributed to the disorderliness in worship which developed in the church at Corinth. Ecstatic utterance or "speaking with tongues" brought confusion to the church assembly. Paul was patient with these disturbers. He recognized that they were earnest and sincere, but counseled: "If you in a tongue utter speech that is not intelligible, how will anyone know what is said? For you will be speaking into the air. There are doubtless many different languages in the world, and none is without meaning; but if I do not know the meaning of the language, I shall be a foreigner to the speaker and the speaker a foreigner to me. So with yourselves; since you are eager for manifestations of the Spirit, strive to excel in building up the church" (1 Cor. 14:9-12). The apostle was patient toward the men who created confusion, but he categorically commanded that freedom in worship is to be under the guiding principle that "all things should be done decently and in order" (v. 40).

How much "order" is necessary if worship is to be carried on "decently" or becomingly? The history of worship indicates that "order" came to be more elaborate and fixed. One of the earliest documents extant, uncertain as to date but very near the apostolic period, is the *Didaché*, "The Teaching of the Twelve Apostles." In it are given instructions concerning the observance of the Lord's Supper or Eucharist. Prayers are given to be used in blessing first the cup and then the bread. It is commanded that "no one eat or drink of your eucharist but those baptized in the Name of the Lord, for it was concerning this that the Lord said, 'Do not give that which is holy to the dogs.' " After the observance is a somewhat lengthy prayer of thanksgiving, of exaltation, of confession, and of intercession for the church. The prayer closes with the benediction: "May grace come, and this world pass away. Hosanna to the God of David! If any one be holy, let him come; if any one be not, let him repent. Maranatha. Amen." Wednesday and Friday are mentioned as fast days and Sunday is indicated as the proper day for the celebration of the Supper.

Justin Martyr wrote his *Apology* or defense of Christianity to the Emperor Antoninus Pius about A.D. 140. In this account he gave a description of the worship of the time. Much attention was given to the celebration of the Eucharist or Lord's Supper. After the prayers, members saluted one another with a kiss. The presiding officer then took the bread and wine, offered praise in the name of the Trinity and gave thanks, to which the people cried aloud, Amen. The deacons distributed the elements to all who were present and later carried the bread and wine to those who were absent. It is clearly stated that no one has the right to partake except a baptized believer who lives as Christ commanded.

Justin described the Sunday service: The people assemble and the memoirs of the apostles or the writings of the prophets are read; the president then instructs and encourages the people to practice the truths contained in the Scriptures; he then leads in prayers to which the people respond with Amen. It is obvious that the "order of service" had become somewhat fixed.

During the third and fourth centuries "orders of services" began to take the form of liturgies. By the fourth century worship in the Western church followed this generally accepted form:

The Liturgy of the Word

Lections: Law, Prophets, Epistles, Acts
Gospels, Letters from bishops
Psalms sung by cantors between the lections

Alleluias
Sermon or sermons
Deacon's litany for catechumens and penitents
Dismissal of all but the faithful

The Liturgy of the Upper Room

Deacon's litany for the faithful, with dip-
    tychs (lists of names) of living and dead
Kiss of peace
Offertory: Collection of alms
    Presentation of elements
    Preparation of elements and ad-
        mixture of water to wine
Sursum corda
Consecration Prayer:
    Preface: Thanksgiving and adoration for
        creation, etc.
Sanctus
Thanksgiving for redemption
Words of Institution
Anamnesis
Epiclesis
Great Intercession for living and dead
Lord's Prayer
Fraction
Elevation—'Holy things to the holy'—and
    Delivery
Communion of all in both kinds, each com-
    municant replying Amen; during reception
    Psalms xliii and xxxiv were sung by cantors
Post-communion Thanksgiving
Deacon's litany and celebrant's brief
    Intercession
Reservation of bread only, for sick and absent
Dismissal[1]

The next ten centuries, both in the West and in the East, witnessed the further elaboration and prescription of liturgies. Baptism,
usually of infants, was the sacrament which cleansed from original
sin and made the one baptized a Christian, a child of God, and an
heir of heaven. In the present form, the Roman Catholic ceremonies

at the baptism of an infant call for the presentation of the child at the font by the sponsors. "The priest wears a surplice and a purple stole. He inquires: '————, what dost thou ask of the Church of God?' The sponsors answer for the child: 'Faith.' 'What does faith bring thee to?' 'Life everlasting.' "

The priest breathes on the face of the child; he makes the sign of the cross on the forehead and breast of the child; he places his hand on the head of the child; a small quantity of salt is put into the mouth of the child; the exorcisms are read, to free the child from the dominion of Satan; the priest's stole is laid on the infant. The profession of faith, that is, the Apostles' Creed, is recited by the sponsors and the priest. The priest moistens his finger with saliva and touches the ears and nostrils of the child, saying: "*Ephphatha,* be thou opened!" After the vows or baptismal promises are made, the infant is anointed with the oil of catechumens. The sponsors hold the child over the font, and the priest pours the baptismal water on its head three times in the form of a cross. The child's head is then anointed with holy chrism in the form of a cross. A white cloth is draped over the child's head and a lighted candle is placed in the hands of the sponsors. The name of a saint is usually given in baptism, that the person baptized may have that saint as his intercessor and model.

More important than baptism in Roman Catholic worship is the holy sacrifice of the Mass. The Mass is defined as "the unbloody sacrifice of the body and blood of Christ." Latin is the language of the Mass throughout the greater part of the world. The word is from the Latin *missa,* signifying a sending away, a dismissal. The ceremony came at the close of the service, after which the people were dismissed, hence the dismissal or "mass" came to denote the service itself. In the course of time the Mass, with fixed and elaborate ritual, came to be the central act of worship in the Roman Catholic Church.

The ceremony begins with prayers said at the foot of the altar steps. Chants and music include the *Kyrie eleison* ("Lord, have mercy"), the *Gloria,* the collects, Scripture reading, the sermon, the recitation of the creed, the offertory, the *Lavabo* or washing of the priest's fingers, the secret prayers, the *Preface* or real beginning of the observance, the *Sanctus* sung by the choir, and finally the Canon of the Mass. The priest pronounces the words of consecration over the bread, elevates the sacred host and then the chalice containing the wine. After moments of silent prayer for those present and for the dead, the *Pater Noster* ("Our Father") is said by the priest, followed by the *Agnus Dei* ("Lamb of God"). The priest receives the bread and afterward the wine. The communicants come forward and the bread is placed by the priest on the tongue of each. The priest then dismisses the people with the words *Ite, missa est* ("Go, it is the dismissal").

Other Roman Catholic ceremonies are provided for various occasions—confirmation, marriage, extreme unction, ordination. Orders of services are provided for many special occasions—funerals, saints' days, holy days, lent, Passion Week, Easter, and so on. Within the Catholic system, provision is made for the religious observance of almost all the events of life and death. Nothing is left to congregational initiative. The *Prayer Book* contains all needed materials and instructions for the guidance of the worshiping congregation. The Roman system is well called the *hierarchy*, for it is all under the government of the priesthood. The people participate but only as they are directed.

It would be vain to assert that this system of worship is without power. The earnest and faithful adherent would point to many satisfactions received from liturgical worship. Such a worshiper would speak of his delight in its richness and colorfulness. He would express satisfaction in the ancient authority of the Church and its sacraments. He would point to the superiority of the rituals as compared with the shallowness of extemporaneous worship services that depend on the mood and ability of the minister. He would contrast the reverence and quiet of the Catholic congregation with the carelessness concerning sacred things often evidenced in a Protestant church service. He might well point to the long history of the Mother Church, with its vast numbers of adherents throughout the world and its many institutions for human welfare. He might convincingly call attention to the fact that many non-Catholic churches have imitated the Roman liturgies with modifications that have not always brought improvement.

Granted that stately and impressive liturgies have elements of power, the question may be asked, power for what? Is there power for witness that wins the lost to Christ? Is there power for edification that builds up the Christian in grace and virtue? Is there power to sustain vital fellowship with God and with fellow Christians? Is power provided to meet life needs and solve life problems? Is there power for the transformation of an evil social order? It is not enough that liturgical worship serves to maintain and even advance a worldwide ecclesiastical system. May we not conclude that the Catholic concept and practice of worship, whether in the Roman Church or its derivatives, hinders rather than promotes true worship?

Swinging to the opposite pole, there are those who reject form in worship. Notable among Christian groups who turned away from formalism to Spirit-led worship were the followers of George Fox (1624-1691), known as the Society of Friends or Quakers. Fox and his followers became dissatisfied with the formalism and legalism of the Church of England. In his youth Fox was given to wandering throughout the countryside, absorbed in reveries. He was apprenticed to a shoemaker but at the age of nineteen felt a divine call to reform the worship of the Anglican church. He denied the finality of the Bible as the source of divine truth and more than once was imprisoned for heresy and for disturbing worship. He claimed that he had received an "inner light" that transcended the Scriptures and made unnecessary church ceremonials as means of worship. He soon gained followers, who renounced the church and its sacerdotalism and sacramentalism, preferring to be known simply as "the Society of Friends." They were called Quakers in derision, possibly because they trembled at the word of the Lord.

Quakers illustrate worship devoid of form. They neither baptize nor observe the Lord's Supper. As a rule, when they meet in an unadorned church house they sit in silence until someone is "moved by the Spirit" to pray, or to lead a song, or to read a passage of Scripture, or to preach. Silence in the worship service is impressive but can become oppressive and unattractive. It is evident that while ornateness is a hindrance to worship, formlessness is equally an impediment.

One of the gravest hindrances to worship is the modern decline of Sunday as the day of worship. Sabbath observance was placed high in the requirements of the Mosaic law. The penalty for sabbath breaking was extremely severe: "Whoever does any work on the sabbath day shall be put to death" (Ex. 31:15). When Jesus came, he found the sabbath burdened with so many regulatory laws that it had lost its meaning and value as a day of rest and worship. He deliberately violated some of these man-made rules, declaring that "the Son of man is lord of the sabbath" (Matt. 12:8), and stating the Christian principle, "the sabbath was made for man, not man for the sabbath" (Mark 2:27). For this and other reasons the Jewish religious leaders hated him and conspired to secure his death. The resurrection of Jesus on the first day of the week (Sunday) brought about the gradual change from observance of the seventh day to the observance of the first day of the week as the day of rest and worship.

Strict observance of the day was enforced throughout Christendom during the early and middle centuries. The modern era brought revolutionary changes. The so-called "blue laws" requiring strict Sunday observance in the colonies were repealed or went by default with constitutional separation of church and state, growing secularism, and increased Sunday attractions. Urban conditions more and more demanded Sunday labor and laws permitting "works of necessity" were enacted. Gradually Sunday became a holiday for many and a working day for others.

Jesus recognized that rigid and burdensome laws concerning sabbath observance were wrong and a hindrance to its purpose as a day of rest, worship, and humanitarian service. We are now confronted with the other extreme—the loss to the multitudes of the sense of sacredness of Sunday. State and municipal laws continue to exist on statute books and their validity has been upheld by the United States Supreme Court, not because Sunday as a day of rest favors religion and its institutions but because such a day contributes to personal and social welfare. Ministers and churches generally protest Sunday violations, not in the interest of church attendance, but on moral and social grounds.

It is clear that if the churches are to attract people to their services it must be without the benefit of legislation. If Sunday is to be kept as a day of worship, it must be done through persuasion rather than through coercion. Yet the sanctity of the Lord's day remains written in the constitution of the moral universe and its loss is a grave menace to worship. Not for their own advantage primarily but for the sake of individuals and society and for the fulfilment of the divine purpose in the establishment of the day, churches of all faiths should seek to restore and maintain voluntary observance of one day in seven for rest and worship.

Today's churches are confronted with unparalleled competition for the interest, time, and support of the public. Notwithstanding release from long hours of labor, with consequent increased leisure, typical man is under pressure all the time. His shortened hours leave time that is claimed by a multitude of activities. Usually living at a distance from his work, an hour or more may be required for transportation. Reading the daily newspaper will take another hour. An hour will ordinarily be consumed in listening to the radio and a couple of hours viewing television. To keep up with current magazines and books will absorb half an hour or more a day. Theater attendance and observing and participating in sports will require on the average another half-hour or more a day. Pleasure trips in the car on weekends and vacations will add up to at least an hour a day. Home ownership requires care of house and yard, to which not less than an hour a day must be devoted. If eight hours are given to occupation or profession and eight hours to eating and sleeping, our typical American, Christian though he be, has a scant hour a week left for church! If he is not a Christian or if his church loyalty is weak, he finds himself without any time whatever for church attendance.

Tensions that build up for "the organization man" and "the status seeker" are destructive of peace of mind and rest of soul. He needs desperately the strength that comes from worship but tragically he is deprived of the fulfilment of his need by the circumstances of life.

It may come about that church attendance increases rather than relieves the tensions. Matthew's description aptly applies to the crowds to be seen on today's busy streets: "When he [Jesus] saw the crowds, he had compassion for them, because they were harassed and helpless, like sheep without a shepherd" (Matt. 9:36).

"The world is too much with us," said Wordsworth. If this was true in the poet's day a century ago, how much truer it is today! From every quarter stimulation pours in that deepens concern for the world that now is. One result is chronic and unrelieved anxiety. The anxiety may be vague and generalized or it may be acute and specific. Such chronic anxiety grows out of fear that increases fear. There is deep need of trust but in its stead is mounting terror. Once those were called fanatics who looked for a catastrophic end of the world. Now those who forecast such an eventuality are the scientists and statesmen. Some moderns turn to ancient fatalism; "What is to be, will be"—so why worry? Others turn to the scientists, bravely but blindly hoping that such instruments of destruction will be devised that no nation will dare to use them. Others pin their faith to national leaders who, they assume, will somehow find a way out. Others escape into pessimism or into neurotic unreality, either of which is an acknowledgment of defeat.

Turning from the American scene, where in general there is a friendly attitude toward the church and its worship, we look abroad to discover a powerful ideology that is openly hostile. Communism, representing the vast Soviet Republic, repudiates religion as "the opium of the people," denies the authority of the Bible, demythologizes Jesus Christ, and avowedly seeks the destruction of the Christian church as an institution. Worship services, under surveillance, are permitted but teaching and evangelism are forbidden. Communist leaders clearly see that if Christianity succeeds they must fail and that they must root out organized Christianity if they maintain themselves. After a half century, communism now has a generation of adherents thoroughly indoctrinated in its beliefs and practices. To the extent that its ideologies prevail, Christian worship will be threatened if not destroyed. It is claimed that approximately one third of the population of the world is now under Communist domination. To the extent that Christian worship declines, the extent of Communist conquest will be enlarged.

Worship in and of itself, as we have seen, posesses no magic power. Vital worship relates men to God, the source of p through men his power may be made manifest. The res worship to its original purity and power is important f maintaining the prosperity of the churches—it is at the h solution of the problem of human survival.

4

Clarifying
the Meaning and Purpose
of Worship

A missionary in Japan, who had struck up a friendship with a neighboring Buddhist priest, attended the Buddhist worship service. After the service he asked the priest, "In the ritual of worship, why did you do this and that? What was the purpose of your worship?" The priest was puzzled. "Meaning? purpose?" he echoed. "I did what the priest did before me and he did what the priest before him did, as far back as man's memory goes."

The Buddhist's question is pertinent for Christian worship: must it have meaning and purpose? Purposeless worship we may reject, but may not worship be too utilitarian? Two travelers, one a European and the other an American, stood at sunset on the deck of a ship as it made its way through the blue Pacific. "How marvelously beautiful!" exclaimed the European. "Does it not remind you of the greatness of God?" "Yes," replied the American, "but I hate to see all this water going to waste."

Is worship for its own sake? Is it to please God? Is it to benefit man? What takes place when the worshiper worships? Does it make any difference to God? Does it have any effect on man and his affairs? During a long period of "silent prayer," a tired little girl said in a stage whisper, "Mother, is this doing anybody any good?" The question persists: What is the meaning of worship and what is its purpose?

Worship defies dictionary definition. The original English word was spelled *worthshippe*, meaning that to which is ascribed highest worth. A dignitary of church or state is sometimes addressed as "Your Worship" in recognition of his high position. A Greek word translated "worship" in the New Testament is *proskuneō*, meaning "to kiss the hand." To worship thus was to pay homage to a superior, especially when asking of him a favor. This meaning of worship is illustrated when the mother of the sons of Zebedee came to him, "and kneeling before him she asked him for something" (Matt. 20:20). In the Gospels, the worship of Jesus is often associated with some request made of him.

In the Old Testament, the Hebrew word most frequently used for worship is *shachah*, "to bow down." The word pictures the worshiper as prostrating himself in the presence of the majesty and holiness of Jehovah. Abraham's servant, in recognition of the guidance of God that led him to Rebecca in his search for a wife for Isaac, "bowed his head and worshiped the Lord" (Gen. 24:26); and again when Laban and Bethuel agreed to the marriage, Abraham's servant, "bowed himself to the earth before the Lord" (v. 52). The commandment forbidding idolatry speaks of "bowing down" before any images and is preceded by the commandment that Jehovah God shall be the sole and supreme object of worship. Worship throughout the Old Testament is thus conceived as man's attitude of humility in the presence of the mighty and just God and of dependence on the holy and loving God.

Priests were necessary for the leadership of worship and the sacrificial system was given to symbolize the requirements of self-renunciation and repentance and atonement for sin. Many of the Psalms were composed for use in worship that glorified God and gave expression to the worshiper's deep spiritual needs. The priestly "service of the altar" lent itself to abuses when form took the place of content. "The service of the word" was the function of the prophets, who sought to call Israel back to the true meaning and purpose of worship, and who insisted that ethical content should always take precedence over form and ceremony.

Worship in the New Testament brings God near and makes him real. The attributes of God revealed in the Old Testament are assumed—his majesty, holiness, and justice. To this concept Jesus added that of a loving Father as exemplified in himself. When Philip wistfully cried, "Lord, show us the Father, and we shall be satisfied," Jesus replied, "Have I been with you so long, and yet you do not know me, Philip? He who has seen me has seen the Father" (John 14:8-9). Unhesitatingly Jesus declared, "I and the Father are one" (John 10:30). It follows that all we need to know of the Father God we find revealed in his Son Jesus Christ. Paul speaks of the light which shone out of darkness "who has shone in our hearts to give the light of the knowledge of the glory of God in the face of Christ" (2 Cor. 4:6). Peter epitomizes the life and work of Jesus as one who "went about doing good" (Acts 10:38).

Worship in the New Testament is inseparably related to service. When tempted by Satan to worship him, and thereby receive world rulership, Jesus answered by quoting from Deuteronomy 6:13: "It is written, You shall worship the Lord your God, and him only shall you serve" (Luke 4:8). This Old Testament ideal of worship through service Jesus himself exemplified. "I am among you," he declared, "as one who serves" (Luke 22:27). He made service the mark of discipleship: "Why do you call me, 'Lord, Lord,' and not do what I tell you?" he asked. He then pictured the man whose house fell before the storm as one who assented to his lordship but did not obey him (Luke 6:46-49). He made service the test of greatness and gave himself as the example: "even as the Son of man came not to be served but to serve, and to give his life as a ransom for many" (Matt. 20:28). In the final judgment, the credentials of the saved will not be their professions and lip service, but their service of Christ in serving others. Upon nominal worshipers will be pronounced the sentence, "Depart from me, . . . for I was hungry and you gave me no food, I was thirsty and you gave me no drink, I was a stranger and you did not welcome me, naked and you did not clothe me, sick and in prison and you did not visit me. . . . And they will go away into eternal punishment (Matt. 25:41-46).

Worship is often referred to as a "service." Does God count as a service to him a meeting together of Christians to sing, pray, read the Scriptures, give their tithes and offerings, and listen to a sermon? We may well believe that he does. Over and over the psalmist summons God's people to worship him. Language is almost exhausted in the appeals to come into God's presence to praise, to pray, to rejoice, to make an offering, to give thanks, to bear testimony, to listen to his voice, and obey his commandments. The psalmist exhorted: "Offer to God a sacrifice of thanksgiving, and pay your vows to the Most High." God is represented as replying, "call upon me in the day of trouble; I will deliver you, and you shall glorify me" (Psalm 50:14-15).

The first Christians at Jerusalem are pictured as attending the Temple services together daily, "praising God and having favor with all the people." That God was pleased is indicated by the consequence: "the Lord added to their number day by day those who were being saved" (Acts 2:46-47). Paul indicated that singing is an essential element of public worship. He urged the Ephesian Christians not to be filled with wine but to be "filled with the Spirit, addressing one another in psalms and hymns and spiritual songs, singing and making melody to the Lord with all your heart, always and for everything giving thanks in the name of our Lord Jesus Christ to God the Father" (Eph. 5:18-20). His appeal to the Colossians sets forth the ideal of a service of worship pleasing to God: "Let the word of Christ dwell in you richly, as you teach and admonish one another in all wisdom, and as you sing psalms and hymns and spiritual songs with thankfulness in your hearts to God. And whatever you do, in word or deed, do everything in the name of the Lord Jesus, giving thanks to God the Father through him" (Col. 3:16-17).

The book of Revelation is full of descriptions of the worship of God, on earth and in heaven, that is for his sake and glory, without thought of "practical" purpose. The elders and creatures before the throne of God are portrayed as worshiping the Lamb and singing a new song: "Worthy art thou to take the scroll and to open its seals" (Rev. 5:9); and before the throne of God stands the unnumbered multitude of the saved, worshiping the Lamb, while the angels fall on their faces before the throne of God, saying, "Amen! Blessing and glory and wisdom and thanksgiving and honor and power and might be to our God" (Rev. 7:12).

Granting that worship pleases God and is a service to him, it is also true that worship is for the sake of man. What values come to the worshiper? Wherein is he enriched because he has bowed down before his Maker? What increase in the abundance of life has come because man has interrupted his daily routine to recognize the supreme worth of God, to praise him for his goodness, to meditate on his holiness, to renew devotion to his service? What difference does it make in the life of the Christian that he has assembled with others to claim anew the presence of Jesus Christ, to seek a deeper understanding of his will and purpose, and to renew his pledges of love and loyalty? What remaking of life may be expected because worship has led through repentance to reassurance, thence to dedication of life and a recovery of personal resolution and social responsibility?

The truth is that many attend church services with little expectation of these values. Those who plan and lead services of worship should continuously ask, What values will come to those who attend and participate? Unless values are consciously sought, they will in large measure be missed. How may these values be defined?

Worship provides an occasion of fellowship. Man is essentially a social being. Isolation is intolerable. As deep as life itself is the gregarious instinct. This deep desire for togetherness gives rise to countless occasions of meetings for innumerable purposes. The family represents the closest knit unit of such togetherness. Community interests of many kinds call people together. An essential element in the enjoyment of the theater, the concert, the lecture, the sporting event, the parade, or any other such affair is the presence of others. Imagine attending as a lone spectator!

Attending a service of worship provides deep satisfaction for this need of fellowship. Other occasions may bind attendants together in loose bonds or none at all; a service of worship ideally brings together those who are "of the same mind, having the same love, being in full accord and of one mind" (Phil. 2:2). Those who thus come together are reminded to "do nothing from selfishness or conceit, but in humility count others better than [themselves]," obeying the exhortation, "Let each of you look not only to his own interests, but also to the interests of others" (vv. 3-4). In the fellowship of such a group is to be found fulfilment of this deep need of persons for one another.

Worship enhances the sense of individual worth and responsibility. In today's world there may be too much togetherness. The individual gets lost in the crowd. The workman on the crowded assembly line may come to feel that he is just a part of the machinery. The office worker or executive becomes merged with the organization. The teacher is a member of the faculty and the student a part of the student body. The bus rider is just one of the passengers, the shopper is just another customer, the telephone subscriber is just another number in the directory. Members of the family, with their diverse interests, may be almost strangers to one another and the names of neighbors on a crowded street may not be known. The individual in the congestion of the modern city may come to feel that as a person he does not count and that what he does with his life is of little consequence.

Participation in a worship service restores the sense of personhood. In the church one is recognized and welcomed for one's own sake. In the smaller church groups there is a place of responsibility and the absentee is missed. In the larger worshiping congregation, the individual is made aware of his worth to God as well as to his church. Sin and guilt are disclosed as bringing personal alienation from God and repentance and forgiveness bring restoration on a personal plane. The question of Christ is heard and answered, "Of how much more value is a man than a sheep!" (Matt. 12:12), for in worship it is discovered that one person outweighs in value all material things.

Worship gives perspective. Life easily gets out of focus. In a materialistic philosophy, a man's life does consist in the abundance of things possessed. The rich farmer in the parable is said to have talked to himself, saying, "Soul, you have ample goods laid up for many years; take your ease, eat, drink, be merry" (Luke 12:19). To this view many a modern retired man would give hearty assent! God pronounced him a fool because he lacked perspective, "This night your soul is required of you," came the verdict; "and the things you have prepared, whose will they be?" Arrestingly, Jesus then declared, "So is he who lays up treasure for himself, and is not rich toward God" (vv. 20-21).

Worship reminds the worshiper of his finitude, the brevity of his life, the need of more than material things to make life worthwhile. In worship, anxieties concerning the necessities of life—food, drink, clothing, shelter—become manifestly useless. In worship the questions that consume so much energy, "What shall we eat? What shall we drink? What shall we wear?" lose their sense of immediacy and importance. Life gains perspective and the truth of Jesus' words is realized: "Seek first his kingdom and his righteousness, and all these things shall be yours as well. Therefore do not be anxious about tomorrow, for tomorrow will be anxious for itself. Let the day's own trouble be sufficient for the day" (Matt. 6:33-34).

Worship is redemptive. Over against God's holiness is man's sinfulness. Sin is the tragic fact of human existence. Sin is not just a theological concept, it is a stark reality. If there is a dark line in God's face, it must be due to the hurt which has come because those whom he made in his image, to have fellowship with him on earth and to live with him forever, have been lost to him. Early in human history it is recorded that "the Lord saw that the wickedness of man was great in the earth, and that every imagination of the thoughts of his heart was only evil continually. And the Lord was sorry that he had made man on the earth, and it grieved him to his heart" (Gen. 6:5-6).

One of the saddest aspects of sin is that so many sinners do not recognize it as grieving God. Paul gave himself as an example of one who committed deadly sin without realizing his offense against God. In his persecution of Christians to the death, he felt that he was doing the service of God. He did not realize his sinfulness until he confronted Jesus Christ, whom he persecuted in persecuting his followers. He did not understand the conflict between good and evil that went on within him until it was revealed to him through Christ's interpretation and exemplification of righteousness. Then it was that he, formerly the self-righteous Pharisee, could confess that Jesus came into the world to save sinners and to say humbly, "I am the foremost" (1 Tim. 1:15).

J. R. Nelson speaks of the church as "the realm of redemption."[1] The church does not save but it is within the realm of the church that Christ's salvation is made known and received. Worship discloses the ugliness of sin and the need of a Saviour. After the sinner is saved, worship rebukes the Christian's failures and selfishness as the white light of God's holiness in Christ reveals sin spots that need cleansing.

Isaiah's experience is typical. He was in the Temple when he saw the Lord, high and lifted up and heard the seraphim chanting, "Holy, holy, holy is the Lord of hosts; the whole earth is full of his glory" (Isa. 6:3). The vision of God's holiness disclosed to Isaiah his sinfulness and when he cried out in dismay one of the seraphim touched his lips with a burning coal taken from the altar and said to the penitent young man, "Behold, this has touched your lips; your guilt is taken away, and your sin is forgiven" (Isa. 6:7). Worship is feeble and of little value unless it has this redemptive element, according to which the sinner finds salvation and the Christian experiences purification.

Worship is educative. The disciples recognized their need of instruction in worship when they came to Jesus with the request, "Lord, teach us to pray" (Luke 11:1). To worship is to experience; to learn is to experience. Worship, therefore, results in learning and learning is necessary to worshiping. If worship is an art, as we must agree it is, the successful conduct of worship and participation in worship requires an artist, and the artist must be a student. The psalmist recognized the need to be taught and that God himself was the great teacher:

> One thing have I asked of the Lord,
>   that will I seek after;
> that I may dwell in the house of the Lord
>   all the days of my life,
> to behold the beauty of the Lord,
>   and to inquire in his temple. ...
> Teach me thy way, O Lord;
>   and lead me on a level path
>   because of my enemies (Psalm 27:4-11).

Teach me thy way, O Lord,
that I may walk in thy truth;
unite my heart to fear thy name.
I give thanks to thee, O Lord my
God, with my whole heart,
and I will glorify thy name for
ever (Psalm 86:11-12).

John Dewey[2] insisted that teaching is guidance and enrichment of experience. Is this not an apt description of leadership of worship? Teaching and preaching may result in knowing *about* God. Worship results in *knowing* God. Teaching and preaching are not thus depreciated, for these activities become more vital and meaningful when teacher and preacher are lost to sight and God's presence becomes real. Worship makes teaching and preaching come alive.

Paul relates worshiping and learning in his prayer for the Ephesian Christians: "that Christ may dwell in your hearts through faith; that you, being rooted and grounded in love, may have power to comprehend with all the saints what is the breadth and length and height and depth, and to know the love of Christ which surpasses knowledge, that you may be filled with all the fulness of God" (Eph. 3:17-19). This knowing Christ, Paul says, goes beyond the *gnosis* that represents humanly acquired knowledge and becomes *epignosis,* the fulness of knowledge which comes through worship.

It is related that James Martineau once counseled a man whose faith was slipping to go to the Black Forest and live for a while among the peasants; then to return to Berlin and live for a while with the city sophisticates. The man so counseled was to observe the ways of worship of both groups and what it meant to their lives. On his return he reported to his mentor that the backwoodsmen, with their simple faith and worship, had a surer grasp of life, made quicker and better decisions, and lived more richly and fully than their sophisticated city contemporaries. The people of the forest had learned through direct communion with God what the people of the city had failed to learn. Worship is a source of truest education.

Worship enriches personality and strengthens character. Personality represents totality of being gathered about a controlling center. Its equivalent in biblical literature is spirit, soul, life. In the Genesis account, "God formed man of dust from the ground, and breathed into his nostrils the breath of life; and man became a living being" (Gen. 2:7). A man's spirit is that which characterizes him and distinguishes him from another, as when it is recorded that "Joshua the son of Nun was full of the spirit of wisdom" (Deut. 34:9); and as that imperishable part of man which "returns to God who gave it" (Eccl. 12:7).

When Jesus spoke of life, the word he used might well be translated personality. "What will it profit a man if he gains the whole world and forfeits his life? Or what shall a man give in return for his life?" (Matt. 16:26). Personality represents the total integration of physical, mental, social, moral, and spiritual qualities of the human being. Character represents this integrated totality as it is employed among men and is judged by them. A gangster may have achieved a high degree of integration and effective personality; yet, as judged by moral and social standards, he is a bad character. A high function of worship is to bring about this integration of the whole of life about God in Christ as the center so that character will be developed under the will of God for the service and welfare of others.

The experience of Christian worship does just that. It makes men whole and sends them out to live and serve with honesty, integrity, sincerity, loyalty, and purity. Continuous experiences of worship are the surest guarantee of meeting the condition, "if any one is in Christ, he is a new creation; the old has passed away, behold, the new has come. All this is from God" (2 Cor. 5:17-18). Christlike character develops in experiences of worship when Paul's injunction is obeyed: "Whatever is true, whatever is honorable, whatever is just, whatever is pure, whatever is lovely, whatever is gracious, if there is any excellence, if there is anything worthy of praise, think about these things" (Phil. 4:8).

Worship energizes for service. A church bulletin introduces the order of service with the words "we enter to worship," and concludes with "we leave to serve." A church gathers for worship in

God's house; it then disperses to serve in God's world. Who shall say which is more important? Without worship, there would be little inspiration for service; without service, there would be little value in worship. Worship and service are as the obverse and reverse sides of a coin.

Old Testament worship deteriorated when it became an end in itself. Prophetic condemnation is uttered against Israel: "Because this people draw near with their mouth and honor me with their lips, while their hearts are far from me, and their fear of me is a commandment of men learned by rote" (Isa. 29:13). Pagans are condemned for their idolatry on many counts, divine judgment upon them being "because they exchanged the truth about God for a lie and worshiped and served the creature rather than the Creator" (Rom. 1:25).

Worship is not a substitute for work just as work cannot take the place of worship. Christians are sternly warned against the sin of idleness: "If any one will not work, let him not eat. For we hear that some of you are living in idleness, mere busybodies, not doing any work. Now such persons we command and exhort in the Lord Jesus Christ to do their work in quietness and to earn their own living. Brethren, do not be weary in well-doing" (2 Thess. 3:10-13). A church contributes something of inestimable value when its spirit of worship is carried over into its people's work.

Worship sustains the hope of world peace. "Is war inevitable?" The question is debated with profound seriousness. Until recently the reply was almost unanimous in the affirmative. Always there had been war, it was said, and always there would be. Historical research disclosed the fact that during the four thousand years of recorded history, fewer than three hundred years were free from war.

Bertrand Russell, the brilliant English agnostic, writing on *Why Men Fight,* assumed that all human activity springs from two sources: impulse and desire. Reason is intended to control impulse and desire but in war reason abdicates. Instinct takes over and a whole nation is moved by fear, hate, possessiveness, pride, revenge. Men in power, who love their power, know that they can best be sustained as warlike leaders and the people most easily led into be-

lieving that they can best be protected by following these leaders and
engaging in war. War, it is argued, disturbs the monotony of peace,
it brings out the heroic in men, it is creative and leads to progress.[3]
Those who declare that war is inevitable even quote Jesus Christ,
for did he not say, "you will hear of wars and rumors of wars"
(Matt. 24:6). And did not Paul picture Christian conquest in terms
of warfare: "Put on the whole armor of God," including breastplate,
helmet, and sword (Eph. 6:11-17).

All these arguments for war, both valid and specious, become
ghastly in the presence of the threat of nuclear and chemical warfare. Another world war would bring such destruction as to result
in practical annihilation of the human race. Winston Churchill
stated the doctrine of "the great deterrent" in his last address to the
British Parliament: "After a certain point has been passed, it may
be said that worse things get better. Thus it might be well said that
by process of divine irony we shall have reached the stage in this
story where safety will be the sturdy child of terror and survival the
twin brother of annihilation."

The Old Testament prophets had another answer. Micah and
Isaiah reported almost identical visions of a warless world:

It shall come to pass in the latter days
    that the mountain of the house of the Lord
shall be established as the highest of the mountains,
    and shall be raised above the hills;
and all the nations shall flow to it,
    and many peoples shall come, and say:
"Come, let us go up to the mountain of the Lord,
    to the house of the God of Jacob;
that he may teach us his ways
    and that we may walk in his paths."
For out of Zion shall go forth the law,
    and the word of the Lord from Jerusalem.
He shall judge between the nations,
    and shall decide for many peoples;
and they shall beat their swords into plowshares,
    and their spears into pruning hooks;
nation shall not lift up sword against nation,
    neither shall they learn war any more (Isa. 2:2-4).

Note that this consummation will come when the nations turn their feet to the house of God and in his worship find the way of peace. Jesus Christ came as the Prince of peace, at whose birth the heavenly host sang, "Glory to God in the highest, and on earth peace among men with whom he is pleased!" (Luke 2:14). Paul declared concerning him: "He is our peace, who has made us both one, and has broken down the dividing wall of hostility . . . that he might create in himself one new man in place of the two, so making peace" (Eph. 2:14-15). The most important enterprise in the world, therefore, is to bring all men to the worship of God in Jesus Christ, for thus war will be abolished and human society saved from destruction.

5

Examining Ways of Worship

Orderly and satisfying worship requires adequate and worthy materials of worship. Just as the house of worship will be drab and unattractive if the right materials are not used in its construction, so will the service of worship be poverty-stricken if there is neglect to use the best available materials of worship.

One who has given little attention to the subject will be surprised to discover the extent and variety of materials of worship which have been developed through the ages.

Christian worship, as we have seen, owes much to the literature of the Old Testament. It must be borne in mind that the first Christians continued to attend the services of the Temple and of the synagogues. A break came within the apostolic Christian group when certain Christian Jews insisted that the Jewish ceremonial law must be observed and that the rite of circumcision was essential to salvation. Paul and the missionary-minded party won at least a temporary victory in the conference at Jerusalem, where it was agreed that the burden of observing the Jewish ceremonial law was not to be laid on Gentile Christians (Acts 15). Yet it appears that the Jewish Christians continued to worship largely according to their accustomed fashion.

The bond that bound together the Christian Jews and the non-Christian Jews was their common joy in worship. Charles Heimsath, in *The Genius of Public Worship*, concluded that

the distinctively Christian characteristic of this worship was in its unrestrained joy of experienced grace, rather than in its form. Into the ancient service of prayer, testimony, and praise the new note of the Gospel was infused, a spontaneous and often unbridled utterance of the joyful discovery. In time the reading of the New Testament writings was added to that of the Old Testament Scriptures and distinctive Christian prayers and hymns were introduced. But Protestant worship, and to a lesser degree Catholic, employs today the basic formulas of public devotion which comprise the synagogue service.[1]

The materials of worship of the early Christian churches were taken largely from devotional portions of both the Old and New Testament Scriptures. Large use was made of the Psalms. Almost certainly there was antiphonal singing, as in Psalm 24 and the psalms of ascent (120-134). There were, no doubt, responses of the congregation to the leader of worship, as in Deuteronomy 27.

The reading of the Scriptures and its interpretation in the form of a homily was customary in the synagogue. This is indicated in Luke's account of the visit of Jesus to the Nazareth synagogue, when Jesus read from the prophecy of Isaiah and applied the words to himself (Luke 4:16-30). When Luke recorded that the Jerusalem Christians "devoted themselves to the apostles' teaching and fellowship, to the breaking of bread, and the prayers" (Acts 2:42), he indicated something of an order of services in which "the prayers" may well have been those customarily recited in a synagogue service, as well as extemporaneous prayers offered by those present.

The ceremonies used in observance of baptism and the Lord's Supper were materials of worship in the early churches. The administration of baptism was a simple, impressive, beautiful rite. Always by immersion, baptism symbolized death, burial, resurrection. Paul asked: "Do you not know that all of us who have been baptized into Christ Jesus were baptized into his death?" He then asserted: "We were buried therefore with him by baptism into death, so that as Christ was raised from the dead by the glory of the Father, we too might walk in newness of life" (Rom. 6:3-4). Not until much later did an elaborate ritual gather about this simple ceremony of baptism.

Materials used in the celebration of the Lord's Supper were more elaborate. Paul described the rite in some detail in 1 Corinthians 11. The Supper was not to be confused with the *agape* or love feast. Careful spiritual preparation was to be made for the Supper, with thoughtful self-examination. Paul severely condemned the disorder and misbehavior that sometimes marked the feast and the Supper in the church at Corinth. He gave an order for the observance of the Supper as Jesus himself instituted it, emphasizing the Lord's injunction, "Do this in remembrance of me." He explained its significance and perpetuity, "For as often as you eat this bread and drink the cup, you proclaim the Lord's death until he comes" (1 Cor. 11:24,26). Early in the history of the churches elaborate materials were developed for use in connection with the celebration of the Supper or Eucharist.

The development in the Eastern or Orthodox Church emphasized worship as mystery. Hislop said:

Its atmosphere is that of mysterious wonder as it contemplates the course of the Divine salvation. Its centre is a Divine process rather than a Divine event; its core the Incarnation rather than the Atonement; its emphasis is the Divine Being and Nature rather than the Divine action or word. In short, it is a Christian mystery and it gives to us the fruit of that development which under the dominant direction of the mystery mood interpreted and experienced the great Christian verities.[2]

At the center of the mystery is not the birth or life or death of Christ so much as his resurrection. Typical is the blessing of the offering of grain, in which the prayer concludes with the words, "For Thou art our resurrection and life, O Christ God, and to Thee with Father and Holy Spirit are due glory, rule, and honor."[3] The eucharistic service dramatizes Christ's incarnation, life, death, and resurrection. The worshiper becomes a spectator of this *mysterium tremendum*. The prayer at baptism reads: "Thou who hast enlightened this thy creature (i.e. water), Christ God darting the light of Godhead into this thy servant (the baptized person) hast freed him and cleansed him and justified him and bestowed adoption, graciously grant equal participation of life; vouchsafe to him perpetual incorruptibility."[4]

In the prayer of confession before partaking of the sacrament of the Supper, the congregation recites: "We offer to thee this awesome and bloodless sacrifice, beseeching Thee that Thou wouldst not deal with us after our sins nor reward us according to our iniquities, but according to Thy gentle and unspeakable love toward men passing by and blotting out the handwriting that is against us Thy suppliants."[5]

Again the recital before taking the sacrament: "We worship thee, O Christ, with Thy Good Father and the Holy Ghost, saying, Thou hast come, Thou hast saved us. Amen, Alleluia. Lord, have mercy; Lord, have mercy; Lord, have mercy."[6]

According to Hislop, there are two absolutions—the absolution of the Son and the absolution of the Father. The latter begins, "Lord God Almighty, Healer of our Souls and our bodies and our spirits . . . . Pardon us, forgive us, as the Gracious One and lover of men."[7] The absolution of the Son begins, "Lord Jesus Christ, the only begotten Son and Word of God the Father Who hast broken every bond of our sins through Thy saving, life-giving sufferings, dispense unto . . . us Thy mercy and break all bonds of our sins."[8]

Hislop concluded: "Over the Eastern worship broods the spirit of mystery, whether the worshiper direct his gaze as in the Coptic service to the altar open and visible whereon the mystery is wrought, or as in the Byzantine Rite where the altar is veiled behind whose screen the worshiper knows the priest beseeches the mysterious coming. The hidden things of the spirit are told in ritual."[9]

Sacrifice rather than mystery is the center about which gathers much of the materials of worship of the Western or Roman Church. The mystery of the incarnation and resurrection of Christ appealed to the mystical-minded East. The saving power of the sacrificial death of Christ appealed to the practical-minded West.

The genius of Roman worship is that it is offered to meet needs. God himself needs and desires the worship of his people. Much of the materials of Roman worship is therefore *objective*; that is, God is its object and he is worshiped with little regard for the presence of a worshiping congregation. Thus, prayer was addressed to God for his sake and hearing: "Glory be to God on high, and on earth peace to men of good will. We praise Thee, we bless Thee, we adore Thee, we glorify Thee, we give Thee thanks for Thy great glory, O Lord

God, heavenly King, God the Father Almighty; O Lord Jesus
Christ, the only begotten Son, O Lord God, Lamb of God, Son of
the Father, Who takest away the sins of the world, have mercy upon
us; Who takest away the sins of the world, receive our prayers; Who
sittest at the right hand of the Father, have mercy upon us. For
Thou only art holy; Thou only art Lord; Thou only, O Jesus Christ,
art most high together with the Holy Spirit in the glory of God the
Father."[10]

Most of the Roman Catholic hymns were of the objective type:
the *Magnificat*, the *Te Deum*, the *Sanctus*, the *Adoramus Te*, the
Cantate Domine, the *Gloria in Excelsis Deo*, the *Pater Noster*, the
Alleluias, and many others. Such worship meets the need of God for
adoration and thanksgiving of his children.

In the Roman concept, worship also supplies the needs of men.
First of all is the need of a sustained salvation. Baptism insures the
soul against being ultimately lost, but there can be earthly loss and
there can be loss through prolonged stay in purgatory. What saves
from eternal loss? The bloody sacrifice of Jesus on the cross. What
saves from temporal loss? The repeated unbloody sacrifice of Jesus
in the Mass, when by the miracle of transubstantiation the bread
and the wine become the flesh and blood of Jesus Christ, in the partaking of which by faith the soul is blessed and renewed.

Ceremonies re-enacting the events surrounding and climaxing the
death of Christ stimulated the creative imagination of priests, poets,
and musicians, resulting in a vast accumulation of eucharistic materials of worship. In the miracle of the Mass, when the sacrifice of
Calvary is renewed before the eyes of men, there is realized Christ's
presence and power not only to save but to keep that which he has
saved. Typical is the prayer *Supplices Te:* "We most humbly beseech Thee, Almighty God, to command that these things be borne
by the hands of Thy holy angels to Thine altar on high in the sight of
Thy divine Majesty, that as many of us as at this altar shall partake
of and receive the most Holy Body and Blood of Thy Son may be
filled with every heavenly blessing and grace."[11] Earnestly received,
the Mass may undoubtedly bring to communicants a deep sense of
security and satisfaction.

Beyond the needs of the living are the needs of the dead. Masses said for the dead are believed to lessen the time and pains of purgatory. Prayers for the dead may likewise be efficacious. Indulgences granted through penance by the living may be extended to the departed. Ceremonials were, therefore, devised for the sake of the dead. Witness the prayer taken from the Mass for the dead on All Souls Day: "O God, the creator and redeemer of all the faithful, grant to the souls of Thy servants departed the remission of all their sins that through pious supplications they may obtain the pardon which they have desired. . . . Mercifully look down, O Lord, we beseech Thee, upon this sacrifice which we offer to Thee for the souls of Thy servants, that to those to whom thou didst grant the merit of Christian faith Thou mayest also grant its reward."[12]

Thus Roman Catholic worship, gathering about the sacrificial death of Jesus Christ, is designed to meet every need of life from birth to death and past death through purgatory to the entrance of the soul into heaven. For a thousand years many of the best minds of the Western world were devoted to the development and transmission of forms of worship suited to the implementation of this purpose.

There were reformers before the Reformation, but they aimed more at correction of the abuses of Roman Catholic doctrine and practice than at reform of worship. John Wycliffe and John Huss, a century before Luther, had boldly attacked the papacy, denouncing the practice of indulgences, pilgrimages, the worship of saints, and the doctrine of transubstantiation. The German Mystics, leaders of whom were Master Eckhart, Heinrich Suso, Johannes Tauler, and Thomas á Kempis, sought to break from the ecclesiasticism of Rome and to restore sincere, heartfelt religion. They did not add very significantly to the literature of worship. The Anabaptists sought to go even further than the fifteenth- and sixteenth-century reformers in their repudiation of formalism and in their attack on infant baptism and the union of church and state. They, too, produced little of value in the literature of worship.

The Reformation which bears the name of Martin Luther (1483-1546) had political as well as religious implications. The time was ripe in Germany, and elsewhere, for revolt against the corrupt power and extortionate demands of Rome. Access to the printed Bible greatly forwarded the movement. Luther and his followers realized that they could not reform the Catholic Church, hence they must break with it and form another kind of church. Such a church called for appropriate forms of worship.

Lutheran worship exalts the Bible as the Word of God. Neither mystery nor sacrifice but revelation is its keynote. In modified form the Mass was retained with the doctrine of transubstantiation changed to consubstantiation—the impartation of the presence of the body of Christ in the sacramental elements after their consecration, not as the actual flesh and blood but as the spiritual presence. Rather than a drama enacted on a stage before spectators, the Mass to Luther was a participation of the communicants as a sign of their fellowship and incorporation with Christ and his saints. Baptism was still held as the means by which one is made a child of God and was to be administered to infants, but its administration served as a witness and a parental pledge as well as a saving sacrament. Luther revised the Catholic formularies for baptism and the Mass largely by cutting out the objectionable elements.

The concept of worship as gathering about revelation restored preaching to a central place. While much of Luther's preaching was polemic, it was also exegetical and inspirational. Preaching needed the support of worship, hence the introduction of German hymns. *Ein' Feste Burg* ("A Mighty Fortress") became the battle hymn of the Reformation. In the main, Lutheran hymns were translations from the Latin of Roman Catholic hymns, with modifications to suit the vernacular, and sometimes paraphrased for doctrinal purposes. The Lutheran church in America confronted the same problem of translation from the German into English. In time the chant fell into relative disuse, especially in America, and was replaced by the chorale, "a simple sacred tune sung in unison as by the congregation, in Lutheran service, where the chorale is characterized by a plain, vigorous harmony, and stateliness."[13] The music is a part of the liturgy and is suited to special occasions and the calendar of the church year.

A measure of freedom is permitted the Lutheran minister and the local congregation, but prescribed orders of service are generally followed. The call to worship is followed by the confession of sins led by the minister with responses from the congregation. The introit, usually a metrical song, is sung in preparation for the service which follows and is concluded with the *Gloria Patri*. The *Kyrie* ("Lord, have mercy") is a litany which may be sung or recited and is concluded with the *Gloria in Excelsis,* after which the congregation will sing or say in unison a prayer in exaltation of Jesus Christ. The minister will then say the *collect,* a brief, comprehensive prayer suited to the occasion. The minister will read the appointed Scripture lesson, a portion from the Old Testament and a portion from the New Testament. The *Gradual,* a liturgical anthem sung by the choir, follows. It is appointed that the Nicene Creed be said or sung on all festivals, and whenever there is a communion the Nicene be followed by the Apostles' Creed. Following a congregational hymn, the sermon is preached. The offertory will bring the service to its conclusion unless there is Holy Communion.

The communion follows a simple ritual consisting of prayer of intercession for the church and of thanksgiving for the grace of God shown forth in the atoning death of Christ. The words of institution, as recorded by Paul in 1 Corinthians 11:23-26, are recited. This is followed by the Lord's prayer and the singing of the *Agnus Dei* ("Lamb of God"), after which the communicants present themselves before the altar and receive the holy sacrament. The minister gives to each communicant individually first the bread, saying, "The body of Christ, given for thee"; then the cup, saying, "The blood of Christ, shed for thee." After all have been served, the *Nunc Dimittis* ("Now lettest thou thy servant depart") is said or sung, followed by a prayer litany and concluding with the benediction.

The service as described may vary, but always the objective in Lutheran worship is the revelation of God in Christ through his word to his people that in their participation they may be strengthened in faith and for service.

Luther was more concerned with the nature of worship as revelation than as mystery or sacrifice. John Calvin (1509-64) found the center of worship in the sovereignty of God. The transcendent God is all-powerful, all-wise, all-holy, everywhere present. God is the Creator; man, the creature, who bows in humility and helplessness before his Maker. Luther accepted the authority of the Bible but held that it must be interpreted by experience. Calvin saw in the Bible the revelation of God and his will, to be accepted as authoritative in its entirety. He felt little need of anything outside the Bible as materials of worship.

In the Calvinistic view of worship, therefore, preaching became supremely important. It was through the preaching of the Word that the will of God was to be found by the people. The sermon replaced the Mass in importance and there was something almost sacramental in "the hearing of the Word." Calvin went beyond Luther in his rejection of the ancient rites that enshrined the ideas of mystery and sacrifice. Baptism and the Supper were shorn of saving power and restored to their primitive simplicity. His *Reformed Church* retained the baptism of infants, not on the ground that the rite possessed saving power, but that it recognized the child of believing parents as coming within the covenant relation comparable to circumcision in the Old Testament. The Lord's Supper is not in itself a means of grace but is an acted sermon.

The Presbyterian Church found its highest development in Scotland. John Knox's *Genevan Service Book* introduced new elements and enriched the austere service devised by Calvin. The *Forme of Prayers* introduced new intercessions and prayers of consecration. The Liturgy of the Word provided a simple order of service with the sermon at the center; the Liturgy of the Upper Room furnished a fuller and richer ritual for the observance of the Lord's Supper. Worshipers came to the table to partake. Only later was practice changed, so that the bread and wine were taken by the elders to the people in their pews. The effort of England to enforce conformity to Anglican forms of worship resulted in revolt which ultimately brought about the overthrow of the English king. Finally, the Westminster *Confession of Faith* was produced, together with *The Form of Presbyterial Government* and *Directory for Public Worship,* which in 1645 were accepted by the Scottish Assembly. Singing for a time was chiefly confined to metrical psalms but later music of a more general nature was introduced. The *Book of Common Order*, authorized in 1928, contains suggested materials of worship of high quality, the use of which is left to the discretion of minister and congregation. The modern Presbyterian service of worship combines dignity and simplicity, intellectual content with conviction, orderliness with informality. Its materials are drawn chiefly from the Bible and related sources.

Many tributaries entered the stream of worship of the Church of England to make it eclectic. The immediate origin of the church was the scheme of Henry VIII to have himself declared head of the church so that he might obtain divorce from Katherine of Aragon and marry Anne Boleyn. Subsequently, a subservient Parliament passed a series of acts completely separating the Church of England from Rome. The King became "Protector and only Supreme Head" of the Church of England. First the lesser and then the greater monasteries were suppressed, relics and images were destroyed; yet the Six Articles of 1539 enforced conformity with the chief doctrines of the Catholic Church.

Henry's successor, Edward VI (1547-1553), extended the Reformation to matters of doctrine. The first *Book of Common Prayer* appeared in 1549 and established a uniform service in the English language. Three years later the first book was revised and shortly thereafter the Forty-two Articles, distinctly Calvinistic, were adopted. Under Mary (1553-58) came violent reaction and Catholic worship was restored. Protestant Elizabeth (1558-1603) reversed the policy of Mary, secured the passage of the Act of Uniformity (1559) which authorized a new prayer book and made the Queen the "supreme governor of the church." The Forty-two Articles were revised to become the Thirty-nine Articles. From this time forward the Church of England was Protestant and national.

The *Book of Common Prayer* is the fountainhead of Anglican and (in America) Protestant Episcopal worship. Hislop wrote:

The Book though culled from many fields is no mere compilation. It has an atmosphere all its own and possesses a dignity and a unity worthy of high praise. Neither in Lutheranism nor in the Reformed communion can there be found so rich and so varied a store of liturgical devotion. That the Book has been patient of many and even opposing interpretations is far from being a discredit. The changing thought of men has not simply called forth different interpretations: it has also left its impress on the Book itself.[14]

As in Eastern Orthodox and Roman Catholic worship, Anglican celebration of the Eucharist is of high importance. No longer the Mass in the Catholic sense, yet it is called the Holy Communion, the rite being delineated in rich detail. Like all other Anglican rituals, it is dignified, beautiful, and restrained. The various orders of worship, following largely the Christian year, reflect the tempo of the British mind in its exactness, its orderliness, its logical sequence, its particularity yet comprehensiveness. To an outsider with another temperament, the service may appear to be too "icily regular," without the warmth that should be associated with the experience of worship. Yet to the devout Anglican or Episcopalian, the worship ceremonials, in which the ceremony is incidental, prove deeply satisfying.

The Methodist movement, led by John and Charles Wesley and George Whitefield, sought to supply the missing elements in Anglicanism—personal religious experience and emotion in worship. John Wesley (1703-1791) was brought up in the best traditions of the Church of England. He acted for a while as curate to his minister father at Epworth. While at Oxford, he and his brother Charles formed the Holy Club, in which they sought the deepening of their spiritual lives. Returning from an unfruitful missionary trip to the United States, John Wesley came under the influence of the Moravian Brethren and was deeply impressed with their evangelical piety. An experience at Aldersgate Chapel, where he felt "strangely warmed," started him on his career as an evangelist, practical theologian, reformer of worship, and notable religious organizer. Associated with him was his brother Charles, himself an effective preacher but chiefly noteworthy for the six thousand hymns and gospel songs which he composed.

The "societies" which the Wesleys formed became the powerful

Methodist Church. In the United States it adopted the name, Methodist Episcopal Church. Naturally, there was retained a considerable element of Anglicanism in its worship. The regenerating efficacy of the sacraments is denied, but baptism (by sprinkling) is administered to children whose parents so desire, and who pledge themselves to bring up their children religiously, on the ground that such children are already members of the household of faith and of the kingdom of God. The Lord's Supper is observed as a memorial of Christ's death, who is really present only in the hearts of those who receive him by faith. The ceremonies of baptism and of the Lord's Supper are conducted with a minimum of formality, often in connection with the stated services in which the sermon is central.

Worship services are not prescribed but the *Book of Discipline* and the hymnals contain suggested orders of service which are generally followed. More recently, greater attention has been given to the elaboration and enrichment of worship, with evidences of decline of the original fervor which characterized the earlier Methodist congregations. Some dissident Methodist groups, with "Holiness" tendencies, have split off from the main body of American Methodists and have sought to preserve the emotionalism which characterized the earlier churches.

Churches seeking to restore and maintain the New Testament congregational polity and practice are characterized in their worship by democracy and freedom. Chief among these bodies are Baptists, Congregationalists, Disciples, Pentecostals, and Assemblies of God. Baptists and Congregationalists have led the way in the democratization of worship. In this concept, worship is "of the people, by the people, for the people." The minister, chosen by the local congregation, is usually the leader of worship. A director of music and choir or choirs may have specialized responsibility, but the genius of the worship service is in congregational participation. Baptism is administered and the Lord's Supper observed as "ordinances" rather than as sacraments, since the latter word has come to be associated with power to save.

Baptists hold that baptism and the Supper are symbolic only, that they are rites entrusted to the local congregation for administration, and that believers only may properly receive the ordinances. The rites may be performed with almost no ceremony or they may be surrounded with Scripture reading, music, devotional meditation, and prayer, but there is total absence of the sacramental ideology characteristic of liturgical churches.

In Baptist circles, minister and congregation are wholly free to adopt their own form of worship. Actually, however, certain orders have become familiar and more or less stereotyped. Usually there is an organ prelude while the people are gathering; sometimes a call to worship or the announcement of a hymn; the invocation is followed by another hymn; the Scripture passage is read, followed by the pastoral prayer; announcements are made and the offering is taken; the anthem by the choir immediately precedes the sermon, which is central; the sermon usually closes with an invitation to church membership; reception of members (if any) is by vote of the congregation; the benediction is the signal for dismissal, with postlude that more or less softens the hubbub of friendly conversation that ensues. The materials of worship are almost exclusively the Bible and the hymnbook.

Such congregationally-centered worship may lack stateliness and even decorum, but it has the value of evangelical purposiveness, of initiative and creativeness, of participation and fruitfulness. Swinging as it does to the opposite pole from the Catholic concept and practice of worship, this democratic worship in many quarters is being enriched through more careful planning and the use of more varied materials. Attractive as such worship may be to some, it would perhaps be well to take into account the need for more of the objective and less of the subjective, more of the sense of the presence of God and less of the prominence of the preacher.

6

Planning and Conducting
the Worship Service

The minister or priest of a church committed to the use of a prescribed order of worship is relieved of the necessity of planning the service. He and his associates are provided with a liturgy, usually dated, which for his communion has been universalized and has stood the test of time.

Many advantages are claimed for this type of prepared worship service. It makes use of the accumulated ceremonial wealth of the past, enriched by the Scriptures and classical church music. The prepared service links the present worshipers with those who have gone before and thus revives historical memory. The liturgy saves the congregation from the minister's unpreparedness, whether due to laziness, mediocre ability, or lack of time. It is argued that there must be some form; why not an approved form that has been tried and found worthy through the ages? The leader of worship, relieved of the necessity of devising an order of service, can devote himself to the skilful conduct of the service. The congregation, with the detailed order before them, can follow it with confidence and concentration.

Objections to the liturgical service are many and to the free churchman are convincing. Worship is life, not ceremony, and when worship has been encased in ceremony it tends inevitably to lose vitality. The liturgy dates from the past and worship should be contemporary and relevant. Prescribed worship takes away the liberty of minister and congregation, the liberty of which Jesus spoke when he said, "you will know the truth, and the truth will make you free" (John 8:32); and of which Paul wrote, saying "for freedom

Christ has set us free; stand fast therefore, and do not submit again to a yoke of slavery" (Gal. 5:1).

The history of Christianity indicates that institutionalism and ceremonialism cut the nerve of evangelical zeal, thus robbing worship of its primary purpose, to bring the lost to Christ. Emerson once said, "Every man is as lazy as he dares to be." Minister and congregation need continually to be reminded of the danger of indolence in worship.

Freedom in worship, however, does not mean license. Indeed, freedom puts upon minister and congregation even heavier responsibility for careful planning of the worship service and its orderly and effective conduct. Just as music and other art forms have their regulating principles, so does worship. Boundaries of worship are prescribed by the nature of worship itself. It is a mistake, therefore, to think that freedom in worship means that a premium is placed on unpreparedness, extemporaneousness, noisiness, disorderliness, carelessness. Brenner thus eloquently pleads the case for worship that is acceptable to God and worthy of man:

Worship is what happens when a good man becomes fully aware of the presence and purpose of God. Worship within the church is the co-operative response of the Christian community to that Divine "Presence-Purpose." Whenever Christians have been keenly aware of the real presence and the true purpose of God, the flames upon the altar of their hearts and upon the Altar of the Church have burned brightly and have lighted a way to Him who is "the way, the truth, and the life." Whenever, on the other hand, the opiates of sin have dulled the sensory nerves of the soul, when man's vision of God is dimmed and his consciousness of spiritual things fails him, the flames of worship die down, the altar of the heart grows cold, and man contents himself with playing in the ashes. He worships no more.[1]

Freedom in worship does not mean lawlessness and formlessness. Although free worship rejects the rigidity of the prescribed liturgy, it must conform to inherent laws and obey the requirements of orderly procedure. Just as the spirit of man needs an organized body for its expression, so spiritual worship needs structure. When Jesus said, "God is spirit, and those who worship him must worship in spirit and truth" (John 4:24), he did not mean that worship is without form and order, for the God who is spirit is also God of law and order.

The movement of free worship is from a beginning point through intermediate stages to a destination. Orders of service may vary greatly, but study of a satisfactory worship experience will disclose that there are several well-defined elements. Recognition of these essential parts of the satisfying whole will help avoid haphazardness and confusion in planning the worship service. Stages in the experience of worship may thus be indicated.

Preparation should be made for entrance into worship. The house of worship, as people approach it, should induce a worshipful frame of mind. The location of the building and the grounds on which it stands will share in making worship more satisfying. Just as a residence is made more homelike and inviting if it is set back from the street and is approached through a lawn with shrubbery and flowers, so a church house is made more attractive and inviting if it is not too close to the noisy thoroughfare, and if its site is appropriately landscaped. There is no one type of architecture which can be called "sacred," but a church house should possess a distinctive that marks it off from other buildings. It should be neither too severely plain nor too ornate. The building should be useful for educational and social purposes, but it should be unmistakably distinguished as a place of worship. It is a sanctuary, a place set apart for sacred use, but special emphasis should be placed on that portion of the building where the stated services of worship are held. As the people enter its doors, they should be reminded that they have come for worship.

Preparation requires that the leaders of worship prepare themselves. John Henry Jowett, in his lectures to preachers, warned against the peril of "deadening familiarity with the sublime." He pointed out that "it is possible to be fussily busy about the Holy Place and yet to lose the wondering sense of the Holy Lord."[2]

The minister must realize that it is as important to prepare himself as his sermon. Self-preparation on the part of those who lead the music is equally important. They may have given themselves assiduously to rehearsals and their performance may be of high order, but if they themselves are not imbued with the spirit of worship they will find it difficult, if not impossible, to lead the congregation in worship. The ushers play a greater part than is often realized. They, too, need preparation that comes through prayer, heart-searching, and understanding of their duties.

Members of the congregation need preparation for worship. The most carefully prepared service may be spoiled if the people come noisily into the place of worship, chat with their neighbors during the prelude, sit inattentive and uncooperative, and apparently have little sense of being in God's house and in his presence. Their mood before they leave home, their attitudes in the teaching and training services, their feeling as they enter the auditorium will do much to determine the effectiveness of the service that follows.

Granted preparation, the next stage in the beginning of worship is recognition. Always and everywhere God is present, but in a special sense his presence is recognized at the time and the place of worship. The organ prelude should do more than drown out the noise of the entering congregation—it should be a reminder of the purpose of their assembling and should set the mood for the service.

The "call to worship" should be more than a mere signal that the service is about to begin. Something is lost if the service begins abruptly with the announcement of a hymn. The call to worship should be just that—a focusing of attention on the primary purpose of the assembly. The call may be given by the choir, as the congregation stands; or choir and congregation may join in singing the "Doxology" or the *Sanctus*; or the minister may recite a Scripture passage or an appropriate devotional prose or poetry selection. The call to worship, whether sung or spoken, should not be selected at random but should effectively introduce the theme of the worship service and help to establish its mood. Repetitive singing of the same call to worship tends to become meaningless except as a signal that the worship service has begun.

Recognition of God's presence will then be followed by invocation of his blessing. What is to be said or sung or done is lifted up to him for his guidance, acceptance, and approval. The invocation, addressed to God, should be brief, reverent, and related to the purpose of the service. Following the invocation, with eyes opened and heads erect in adoration, the choir may lead the congregation in the singing of *Gloria* or a similar response of praise.

Preparation and invocation will normally be followed by inspiration and aspiration. To aspire is to desire ardently; in the language of the psalmist, "As the hart panteth after the water brooks, So panteth my soul after thee, O God" (Psalm 42:1, ASV). Worship is more than quiet waiting on God—it is also active seeking after him. Many of the best-loved hymns are expressions of aspiration: "Awake, My Soul"; "More Holiness Give Me"; "Oh, for a Closer Walk with God"; "Purer in Heart, O God"; "We Would See Jesus." Sometimes such songs may seem unrealistic in light of the lives of those who sing them; yet they express and often awaken an idealism that challenges to realization. For this realization, aspiration needs inspiration. Before breath can be breathed out (aspiration) it must be breathed in (inspiration). There is need for longing and there is need for resolution and power to put longing into practice. This need of inspiration is expressed through such notable hymns as "Lead On, O King Eternal"; "Soldiers of Christ, Arise"; "Onward, Christian Soldiers"; "The Son of God Goes Forth to War"; "Truehearted, Wholehearted," and so on. A service of worship would be incomplete that did not give opportunity for expression of aspiration and inspiration.

If God's presence is recognized, his blessing invoked, and the hearts of worshipers turned to him in aspiration and inspiration, there should then be supplied the felt need of communication—God speaking to the worshipers, the worshipers speaking to him. This two-way communication comes through the reading of the Scriptures and prayer. The reading of the Bible should be as if the living God were present speaking his living Word. Careless Bible reading is inexcusable. Nothing that the minister does should receive more careful attention than his reading of the Scriptures. The passage which he reads should have been read and reread, with key words underscored. His pronunciation and enunciation should be natural and correct. The passage need not always be that from which the sermon text is taken, although it is usually related.

Realizing that for many present this will be their only Bible reading for the week, the minister may choose to lead them in reading
responsively or in unison. Usually it is better for congregational reading to be from selections in the hymnbook or from the passage
printed in the bulletin, since many will not have Bibles and others
may have difficulty in finding the place. Generally, the purpose of
this public reading of the Scriptures will be better served if the King
James Version is used, for it carries with it so many sacred associations and possesses such nobility of diction. There are occasions
when a modern version may be used with propriety but the minister
risks serious loss if he uses it habitually. The Authorized King James
will probably remain the standard for services of public worship for
at least another generation.

Should the people be called to open their Bibles and read silently
with the minister? The practice is open to question. There may be a
scramble for Bibles, distraction and loss of time as members of the
congregation locate the passage, and a loss of the quiet reverence
which comes when all eyes are fixed on the minister as he reads ex-
pressively and impressively.

The uppermost consideration in reading the Bible, whether by
the minister alone or with the congregation, is that God is com-
municating his truths through the printed Word. This impression
may be deepened if the people stand while the passage is read. Always the public reading of the Bible should be thought of as an act
of worship. It should, therefore, be done with simplicity, dignity, and
reverence, just as if God himself were present and speaking.

Worship as communication or communion finds in prayer the
counterpart of God speaking through his Word, as the people in turn
speak to God. Customarily, the pastor will lead the people in this
prayer. He is thus not praying privately but representatively. Henry
Sloane Coffin lists essentials of the pastoral prayer: comprehensiveness, orderliness, concreteness, objectivity, freshness in thought and
language, variety, and brevity.[3] The prayer which Jesus taught his
disciples to pray may well serve as a guide to the pastor's leadership
of the public prayer—confident approach, exalted address, reverent
attitude, deep desire, earnest obedience, social consciousness, per-

sonal needs, spiritual needs, guidance needs, deliverance needs, acknowledgment of sovereignty. Each phrase of the prayer may be bracketed with particulars, according to the minister's sense of the longings, problems, and needs of the congregation. With some such outline of prayer before him, the minister may pray vicariously and effectually as he leads the people to pray. He thus will be saved from disconnectedness, rambling, repetitiousness, shallow emotionalism, the confusing of praying with preaching. Obviously, the minister's preparation for praying should be counted fully as important as his preparation for preaching. No other aspect of his leadership is more significant than his leadership of the people in prayer.

The communication of God to his people through his Word and their communion with him through prayer should naturally lead to dedication. Worship reaches a high point in the offering. Sacrifice is an element in all worship—pagan or Christian. Central in Jewish worship was the sacrificial system: the bloody sacrifices and meal offerings, the burnt offerings and communal meal offerings, the sin and guilt offerings. The giving of the tithe for sacred purposes was common to Semitic peoples, combining tribute, gift, thank offering, consecration offering, and support of the priesthood. Religiously inclined men have always felt that a proportion of their resources should be placed at the service of their religion. The tithe for Israel was in the form of a tax, collectable legally. Yet there were many ways of evading it and its intention was fulfilled through voluntary payment as an act of worship. Jesus criticized giving "to be seen of men" but commended the widow who out of love gave all that she had. He condemned legalized tithing that substituted for "justice and mercy and faith"; yet he placed the weight of moral obligation on tithing, saying that this "you ought to have done, without neglecting the others" (Matt. 23:23).

The bringing of tithes and offerings "into the storehouse" as an act of sacrificial worship exalts and pleases God and blesses the worshiper. Like all else in New Testament worship, it should be activated by the spirit of voluntariness. When the money is placed in the offering plate, the giver is giving more than the money—he is giving a part of himself to God the owner for the purposes of Jesus

Christ. The money thus given represents time, talent, energy, skill, thought, life itself. The act of sacrificial giving should, therefore, be observed with appropriate ceremonial. The minister may well speak briefly of the providence of God, the love of Christ, and the guidance of the Holy Spirit which have made possible the possession of material wealth; or, he may call attention to the objects for which the money is given, perhaps singling out some illustration of the blessing conferred by the church's gifts; or, he may call on a church member, by previous arrangement, to bring a brief testimony as to the joy and spiritual benefits which have come from faithfulness in the stewardship of possessions. It is well to remind the congregation occasionally that stewardship includes the giving of time, effort, ability, influence, and all else that one has.

The congregation may then rise and sing an appropriate hymn; or the choir may sing such offering sentences as "All Things Come of Thee"; "We Give Thee But Thine Own"; "All Things Are Thine"; "Grant Us, Lord, the Grace of Giving"; "May the Grace of Christ Our Saviour"; or a similar refrain. During the singing those who are to take the offering will take their places before the pulpit. As the offering is received, piano or organ music may sustain the mood of worship. When the offering plates are returned, the congregation may again stand and sing the "Doxology," "Bless Thou the Gifts," or a similar response. Appropriately now there may be a brief prayer of dedication of the offering led by a deacon, the minister, or other member of his appointment. In all of this there should not be ceremoniousness but the magnifying of the offering as a sacrificial act of worship through which God is glorified.

What of announcements? The fewer the better! Almost any church can afford at least a mimeographed order of service with announcements included. Matters of moment connected with the life and work of the church may of course be brought to the attention of the congregation but promotional sales talk is out of place. Visitors may be welcomed and their names and addresses received on cards quietly distributed but personal introductions and fanfare should be omitted. Such interruptions tend to break the mood of worship which may not thereafter be easily restored.

From the climax of dedication in the offering, worship moves into its final phase of illumination for the sermon. The transition is customarily made through the choral rendering of an anthem, a solo, duet, or quartet. Never should the part of the choir be operatic performance or musical entertainment. The listening congregation should experience the deepening of the mood of exaltation of God in Christ and submission to the guiding presence of the Holy Spirit as the choir sings. The minister should then confront the congregation thus made ready for the climax of the service—the preaching of the sermon.

The sermon is not something apart from the preceding worship activities nor are these activities merely preparatory to the sermon. All the other elements of worship are now caught up and illuminated in worship. The preacher as God's prophet, Christ's interpreter, and the Holy Spirit's instrumentality brings light from the revealed Word for the lives of needy listeners. "Preaching," said Philips Brooks, "is [communication of] truth through personality." If it is not worshipful, preaching misses its meaning and purpose. Preaching is worshipful when it presents to the congregation the will of God, the claims of Christ, the meaning of life, and the challenge to life fulfilment. Sadly, not all preaching is thus God-conscious, Christ-mastered, life-centered.

Norman Cousins, editor of the *Saturday Review*, in an editorial entitled "Ministerial Corn," tells of a conversation with a church-going farmer. It was on a Sunday and the talk turned to church-going and to preachers. The farmer had become interested in why so many of his neighbors did not attend church, notwithstanding that many of them listed themselves as church members. "My theory is," he declared, "that too many ministers can officiate but not preach. The Sunday sermon in too many cases has become little more than an endurance feat for those who have to sit through it." He had visited most of the churches of the community and had studied the sermons heard. He had noted the "singsong" effects achieved by some of the ministers, which left the impression that so much time and effort went into polishing the soundtrack that there was hardly anything left for the meaning. "You almost feel as though you were expected to judge the spiritual value of a sermon by the tonal vibrations." He observed the repetitious sentences, the awkward literary construction, the grammatical errors, the trite and outworn arguments—in a word, the "ministerial corn." The farmer admitted that he found exceptions but in too many cases he was exposed to "a heavy artillery in oratory combined with a blank cartridge in ideas."[4] Obviously such preaching is not worshipful.

The service of worship does not conclude with the sermon. The movement of all the activities preceding leads to the crucial point— the invitation. The invitation is planned and extended with a view of obtaining from the congregation the response of commitment. The invitation may at times be directed to the Christian church members, calling for their commitment or recommitment to truth presented or action demanded. On occasion, the invitation may be to rededication of life in renewal of consecration to Christ. In a church with evangelistic purpose and mission (should there be any other kind?) the high moment of the service is when, earnestly and persuasively, the invitation is given to public profession of repentance toward God and faith in the Lord Jesus Christ—sincere response to which brings assurance of Christ's living presence and power. Reception into the fellowship of the church of those who thus respond brings joy to the Christian family that another member has been added, as when a child has been born into the family circle.

The final movement in the service of worship is summed up in benediction. The benediction should carry with it more than a mere signal of dismissal. It has no such connotation as in the Catholic Mass; nevertheless it is no mere incident, indicating that the people are at liberty to leave. The word carries with it the idea of that which is well spoken, that which pleases God and blesses men. It seeks to clinch the mood, the impulses, the resolutions, and commitments which have been brought about by the service and to give them sustaining power for the days ahead. These closing moments should be marked by silence and deep reverence, following which the signal of dismissal is given by the choral *Amen*. The organ postlude is selected with a view to continuing and sustaining the mood of the total service.

Here are essential elements that enter into the ongoing movement of worship from its reverent beginning to its fruitful conclusion—preparation, recognition, aspiration and inspiration, communication, dedication, illumination, invitation, reception, benediction, and postlude. These movements of worship admit of almost infinite variety but give structure to the order. Obviously such movement to be satisfying must be planned and conducted co-operatively and with prayerful seking for divine guidance.

Committee on building and grounds, caretaker, deacons, and ushers—those responsible for providing an attractive entrance into worship—must work with those responsible for the leadership of worship. Those responsible for the musical aspect of worship must study the congregation's needs and abilities and plan to meet these needs and develop these abilities. Vocalists and instrumentalists must understand and appreciate one another and confer continuously for the improvement of music. The committee on worship (preferred to "music committee") should be keenly aware of excellences to commend and faults to amend in the services as planned and conducted. Staff members should be relied on to discover and suggest changes that would make the worship services more satisfying.

Inescapably, progressive improvement in planning and conducting worship is a responsibility of the pastor-preacher. He must take time from pastoral duties and sermon preparation for guidance of the total service of worship. As he plans the sermon, he should bear in mind the worship activities, making notes of suggestions to be passed on to others who with him are responsible for the service. He, of course, will not undertake to force his ideas on these colleagues, but he will so win their confidence and respect that they will gladly accept him as leader of the worship team. His sermons and their objectives should be determined sufficiently in advance that the director, musician, and choir members may choose appropriate music. His presence occasionally, if not regularly, at choir rehearsals will be time well spent. At no other point of his public ministry will the minister's efforts be more richly rewarded than in prayer, thought, and time given to the effective planning and conducting of the public worship services of his church.

7

Magnifying Music in Worship

Worship and music are inseparable. When the curtain rises on the beginning of things, we hear man communing with God; and in the Genesis account we read of Jubal, "the father of all such as handle the harp and pipe" (Gen. 4:21, ASV). Early in the human story, it is recorded: "The morning stars sang together, and all the sons of God shouted for joy" (Job 38:7).

Various conjectures have been made as to the origin of music. The first music was probably vocal in character. It may have been a modulated cry of joy or pain; or it may have developed from hunting calls, or other vocal signals employed in primitive life. Elson holds that "as soon as such calls were used for the pleasure expressed or imparted, apart from any useful purpose, they became music."[1]

Some authorities associate vocal rhythm with dancing. Primitive worship took the form of action, which was usually accompanied by rhythmic chanting or the beating of some instrument akin to the drum. There is a legend that the Chinese sage, Ling-lun, listened to a bird singing to its mate and invented the diatonic scale by an arrangement of bamboo reeds. Elson supposes that musical instruments were developed from sounds in nature—the whistling wind suggesting the flute; a branch bumping against a hollow tree leading to the drum; the twanging bow string giving rise to the harp. The most ancient instrument, as indicated by prehistoric relics, was a kind of flute. The most highly developed primitive musical instrument was probably the harp.

Very early the Hebrews made use of vocal and instrumental music in worship. The psalmist called on the worshipers of Jehovah to "make a joyful noise," to "break forth and sing for joy," and mentioned the use of the harp, the trumpet, the cornet, along with the human voice (Psalm 98, ASV). The bringing of the ark of the covenant to Jerusalem was celebrated with a great outpouring of vocal and instrumental music: "David also commanded the chiefs of the Levites to appoint their brethren as the singers who should play loudly on musical instruments, on harps and lyres and cymbals, to raise sounds of joy" (1 Chron. 15:16).

Music had a prominent place in the dedication of Solomon's temple: "The priests stood at their posts; the Levites also, with the instruments for music to the Lord which King David had made for giving thanks to the Lord—for his steadfast love endures for ever—whenever David offered praises by their ministry; opposite them the priests sounded trumpets; and all Israel stood" (2 Chron. 7:6). Through the centuries, until the Christian era, music was prominent in Hebrew worship and became immediately a part of the Christian heritage of worship.

The curtain rises on the birth of Christ to singing by the heavenly choir. Luke records in poetic form the announcement of the angel to Zacharias that to him and his wife Elizabeth would be born the Forerunner of the Messiah. The annunciation to Mary is poetic; and when Mary realized that she was to be the mother of the Christ, her amazement, humility, and gladness found expression in pure poetry (Luke 1:32-35,47-55). Later when John was born, the tongue of Zacharias was loosed and his joy poured forth in poetry (Luke 1:68-79). When the Holy Child was brought to the Temple in compliance with Jewish custom and Simeon realized that he was seeing the Lord's Christ, he took the child in his arms and blessed God and broke into song (Luke 2:29-35). These poetic utterances were later set to music and became the precious hymns of the early churches.

The first three centuries witnessed an extraordinary development of Christian music. In it were blended Hebrew, Greek, and Latin elements, but the result was not just a composite but a new musical creation. Douglas points out that:

Within three centuries, the period of experiment, assimilation, and codification has ended with the establishment, in the time of Pope St. Gregory the Great, of the first complete corpus of fully artistic music which the world had ever known, in which the enduring principles of relationship between church music and Catholic worship were perfectly and permanently set forth. . . . Christianity began in a Jewish environment in the midst of a Graeco-Roman culture. In a rapidly changing world, it became a growing force that was to become dominant, and to bring about a unification . . . . in which a perfect fusion of Hebrew, Greek, and Roman elements formed a new embodiment of artistic expression comparable only to the culmination of Greek sculpture in the Periclean age.[2]

When the celebration of the Eucharist became central in Roman Catholic worship, music likewise gathered about this rite. The Mass was preceded by a processional psalm, sung as a solo with a choir refrain. During the offering of the bread and wine, a solo psalm was sung with choir responses. The litany was in the form of dialogue between celebrant and congregation, usually a chant. The congregation's part through song and chant were in the beginning an essential part of the celebration of the Eucharist. Hymns by the congregation were usually confined to the "Kyrie eleison," the "Gloria in Excelsis," and the "Sanctus."

The greatest of the early popes was Gregory (590-604). He consolidated the power of the papacy, established celibacy for the priesthood, sent missionaries to Britain and Germany, and greatly extended the authority of the Roman See. One of his lasting achievements was the systematic collection of forms of worship and his insistence on uniformity of worship throughout Catholic Christendom. Under his direction and patronage, the *schola cantorum* (school of song) was developed for the training of singers and musicians. This institution became the first conservatory and for almost eight hundred years served to produce, improve, and disseminate most of the church music of the Western world. Protestants as well as Catholics are under a deep debt of gratitude for this contribution.

The Roman Church is avowedly a hierarchy—an ecclesiastical empire ruled by priests. According to this concept, only ordained men can perform the offices of the Church. Traditionally, the Church has discouraged the reading of the Scriptures by the people on the ground of their incompetence to interpret aright. The same theory applies to music. Church music is the responsibility of trained priests and choirs. The part of the congregation is to listen reverently and understandingly.

Luther broke with this view and sought to restore music to the congregation. Luther was a musician of no mean ability. He composed a number of hymns and encouraged the composition of a whole group of chorales which form the basis of much Lutheran church music from that time to the present. Luther saw in music a powerful means of indoctrination and in this he was supported by his contemporary, Philipp Melanchthon, who wrote: "When church music ceases to sound, doctrine will disintegrate. Religious music applied to life is a sanctification of life."[3]

Zwingli, on the other hand, undertook to abolish music altogether and to substitute antiphonal recitation of psalms and canticles, although later he grudgingly tolerated congregational singing. Calvin encouraged the singing of simple songs by the people, accompanied by musical instruments. The Puritans of England and Scotland disliked complexity in music and confined themselves to the singing of metrical psalms. Hymns were of human composition, they held, and so were to be avoided as infringing on the authority of the Scriptures. Some early Baptists disliked the use of hymnbooks and forbade the use of instruments in their churches.[4]

A new era in church music dawned in the seventeenth century. Ecclesiastical music in the preceding centuries was in the main incidental to the words. The two morning stars of the musical renaissance were Johann Sebastian Bach (1685-1750) and Georg Friedrich Handel (1685-1759). Born in the same year, these two pioneers have sometimes been called the "Siamese twins of music." While their style of composition differs widely, they are both notable for giving to music itself a high and respected place in the church. They introduced the concert oratorio which in turn led to the enlargement and strengthening of church choirs. Dickinson summed up the contribution of Bach by asserting that he

lent the illuminating power of his art to the ideas which brought forth the Reformation. It is the central demand of Protestantism, the immediate personal access of man to God, which, constituting a new motive in German national music, gave shape and direction to Bach's creative genius. . . . His art touches the deepest chords of religious feeling. . . . His music is not the music of a confession, but of humanity.[5]

Handel is best known of course for his *Messiah,* which combines scriptural materials with solos and choruses of marvelous beauty and impressiveness. This new era was broadened in the eighteenth century by such composers as Christoph von Gluck, Franz Joseph Haydn, Wolfgang Mozart, Ludwig van Beethoven, and Franz Schubert. These masters of music did not confine themselves to religious themes but they vastly enriched church music.

These seventeenth- and eighteenth-century classical composers demonstrated that music has a place in worship in its own right. Appropriate lyrics are, of course, essential but music is more than just a vehicle of thought. Grandeur in music fitly represents the grandeur of God and leads men to recognize his presence and bow before his majesty.

Stateliness in music may induce reverence and awe but it is inadequate in its appeal to the total emotional life. The industrial revolution and the democratic movement elevated the lower and middle classes to a new position of importance. Their spiritual hungers were not met by the formal worship and the stately music of the established churches. The time was ripe for the soul-searching preaching of the Wesleys and Whitefield and the emotion-stirring songs of Charles Wesley and Isaac Watts.

In extolling the leadership of John Wesley, historians have been inclined to neglect the influence of Charles. If John Wesley's monument is the Methodist Church, his brother's monument is the singing churches. When the volume of Charles Wesley's composition is considered—about six thousand songs—it is no wonder that some of them are feeble and dull; but when from this vast volume are extracted such hymns as "Jesus, Lover of My Soul," "Love Divine, All Loves Excelling," "Christ, Whose Glory Fills the Skies," "Hark! The Herald Angels Sing," "Christ the Lord Is Risen Today," "A Charge to Keep I Have," and "Soldiers of Christ, Arise!" perhaps this tribute to the first collected songs of Wesley is not too extravagant: "This little book—some 750 hymns—ranks in Christian literature with the Psalms, the Book of Common Prayer, the Canon of the Mass. In its own way, it is perfect, unapproachable, elemental in its perfection. You cannot alter it except to mar it; it is a work of supreme devotional art by a religious genius."[6] No evangelical hymnal since that time would be considered complete without some of Charles Wesley's hymns.

Isaac Watts, the Congregationalist dissenter, deserves with Charles Wesley credit for the introduction of hymns properly classified as "popular." Watts preceded Wesley by thirty-three years and composed his songs under greater limitations than Wesley. The congregations for whom Watts wrote were on a lower social and educational level. Wesley's hymns are more subjective, Watts' more objective. This is reflected in the greatest of Watts' hymns—one of the greatest in English hymnody—"When I Survey the Wondrous Cross." This characteristic is seen also in such well-known hymns as, "O God, Our Help in Ages Past," "Begin, My Tongue, Some Heavenly Theme," "Before Jehovah's Awful Throne," "Joy to the World! The Lord Is Come," "The Heavens Declare Thy Glory, Lord," "Jesus Shall Reign Where'er the Sun."

A new world of church music was begun with the singable tunes and emotion-charged words of the hymns of Wesley and Watts. The Church of England was slow to join the movement for popularization of the worship service and strongly opposed the Wesleys, who continued to consider themselves Anglicans. However, hymnals began to appear sporadically in Anglican churches, although action was brought against the vicar of St. Paul's by the York consistory court when a popular hymnal was introduced.

The victory was won and the tyranny of the metrical psalms broken with the appearance of the hymns of Reginald Heber (1783-1826). Heber was a man of rare literary ability, which he combined with administrative genius as bishop of all India. In the year following his untimely death, a small volume of his collected hymns was published. The collection included fifty-seven hymns written by Heber himself. Almost all of these hymns remain in use, some of the most familiar of which are, "Brightest and Best of the Sons of the Morning"; "God, That Madest Earth and Heaven"; "From Greenland's Icy Mountains"; "Holy, Holy, Holy"; "The Son of God Goes Forth to War." Contemporary with Heber's collection of hymns was Keble's *The Christian Year,* in which appeared Keble's great hymn, "Sun of My Soul, Thou Saviour Dear" and "There is a Book, Who Runs May Read." From the beginning, the hymnals of the Anglican-Episcopal Church have been organized about the calendar of the church year. These hymnals have been notable for their uniformly high quality of both music and poetry.

Church music in America was at first an inheritance from the Old World. The freedom and expansiveness of the New World was not hospitable to the restraints which characterized much of the church music of England and the Continent. The Wesleyan revival influenced the churches of the United States but indigenous evangelism appeared in the "Great Awakening." Gospel singing became almost as important as gospel preaching in the "revival meeting." A vast output of gospel songs resulted and these have been among the most important contributions to American church music.

In the main, American hymn writers have reflected the spirit of American democracy, liberty, activity, militancy, vitality, evangelistic and missionary zeal, and devotion to Jesus Christ, the Bible, and the church. Hymnody has been enriched by such hymns as Phillips Brooks' "O Little Town of Bethlehem"; Francis Scott Key's "Star-Spangled Banner"; Timothy Dwight's "I Love Thy Kingdom, Lord"; Ray Palmer's "My Faith Looks Up to Thee"; George Doffield, Jr.'s "Stand Up, Stand Up for Jesus"; Samuel Wolcott's "Christ for the World We Sing"; Sarah Adam's "Nearer, My God, to Thee"; Frances Havergal's "I Gave My Life for Thee"; Sylvanus Phelps' "Something for Thee"; Fanny Crosby's almost innumerable songs, among the best loved of which are "Blessed Assurance, Jesus Is Mine," "Jesus, Keep Me Near the Cross," "Praise Him! Praise Him!," "Rescue the Perishing," "Jesus Is Tenderly Calling," and "All the Way My Saviour Leads Me"; Charles Gabriel's "Send the Light!," "More Like the Master," and "Oh, That Will Be Glory"; B. B. McKinney's "Have Faith in God," "Wherever He Leads I'll Go," and many others; Cecil Alexander's "Jesus Calls Us o'er the Tumult"; Philip P. Bliss's "Wonderful Words of Life," "Whosoever Will," "Let the Lower Lights Be Burning."

By no means exhaustive, this almost random sampling of songs represents the type of church music contributed by American poets and composers.

Two types of music are original to the United States—the Negro spiritual and jazz. The spirituals were spontaneous expressions of deep longings of the Negro people during their period of slavery. In them is no bitterness because of their servitude and suffering but a plaintive longing for release as in "Go Down, Moses," deep insight into the meaning of sin as in "Were You There When They Crucified My Lord?" and faith in a better world to come as in "Swing Low, Sweet Chariot." Little is known as to the authorship of the spirituals. Most of them are true folk songs and are, therefore, inimitable. They are still treasured and used by Negro congregations but have had no appreciable influence on American hymnody as a whole.

Jazz is a modernization of primitive animistic music. One of its chief characteristics is syncopation—the broken beat, irregular rhythm, deliberate disharmony. Jazz in its various forms represents the modern quest for the unusual and rebellion against the accepted. To some extent and in some quarters, jazz has influenced church music but the common sense of Christians rejects this form of music as unsuited to the worship of God. Somewhat between the Negro spiritual and jazz is the so-called "hillbilly" type of music, patterned after the folk-singing developed in certain rural areas of the United States, especially in the mountain regions. Gospel songs of this type are tuneful, singable, sentimental; for example: "On the Jericho Road," "I've Had a Little Talk with Jesus," "Farther Along," "Give the World a Smile Each Day," "The Man Upstairs," "When the Saints Go Marching In," and the like. Yet they are not usually thought of as belonging to the historic body of hymnody.

One of the most significant recent developments in American church music is the organized Music Ministry under direction of a qualified minister of music who serves as a staff member. Instead of the one traditional adult choir responsible for leadership of the music at the stated hours of worship, choirs are provided for all age groups, from the "Cherub Choir" for small children to the adult "Sanctuary Choir." Better music is sought for all services of the church and its organizations and is thought of as ministering to the total life of the church. Even the smaller churches that cannot afford a minister of music are more concerned than heretofore to extend the reach of the music program to include all ages and to make music an effective instrumentality in the improvement and enrichment of worship in the church and in the lives of the members.

The choice of music for worship services calls for prayerful appraisal by those who are jointly responsible for leadership. In making the choice, consideration should be given to the present level of music appreciation and ability of the congregation and choir or choirs. If the standard needs to be raised—as very often it does—the approach should be tactfully made through the skilful introduction of hymns of higher quality. Tests of suitable songs may be proposed and selections made on the basis of agreed criteria. For example, a list of songs may be made; then concerning each suggested song these questions may be raised:

Is it singable? Is it within the range of musical ability of choir and congregation?

Is it scriptural? Is the thought in line with and not contrary to the teachings of the Bible?

Has it breadth and depth? Does it reach both Godward and manward, with universal as well as individual appeal?

Is it reverent? Do words and music convey a sense of God's presence and contribute to an attitude of respect?

Is it excellent? Do words and music measure up to a good standard of literary and musical artistry?

Is it useful? Does the song as a whole aid in achieving the planned purpose of the service?

Is it appropriate? Is it suited to the occasion and congruous with other aspects of the service, especially the sermon?

If to a reasonable degree these questions can be answered affirmatively, the song may properly be considered worthy of listing.

A study of the place of music in worship raises the fundamental question: What is its essential purpose? As early as the fourth century Basil the Great, Bishop of Caesarea, theologian and doctor of the church, wrote insightfully:

For when the Holy Spirit saw that mankind was ill-inclined toward virtue and that we were heedless of the righteous life because of our inclination to pleasure, what did He do? He blended the delight of melody with doctrines in order that through the pleasantness and softness of the sound we might unawares receive what was useful in the words, according to the practice of physicians, who, when they give the more bitter draughts to the sick, often smear the rim of the cup with honey.[7]

Music may be used for religious ends, but it is doubtful if any music can be designated *religious* in and of itself. The religious quality of the music inheres in the accompanying words, the occasion of its use, and its purpose. Music is useful as providing a setting for the sermon but this is not its chief purpose. Music may serve to enhance the communication of truth, but again this is an ancillary and not the basic use of music. There is an element of aesthetic enjoyment in music, but music in church should not be just for enjoyment and entertainment. Music may be inspiring and elevating and often is a powerful aid to decision, but these are factors associated with the appeal of the preacher and are concomitant values. Music involves participation of the congregation, either through passive listening or active participation, but the value of participation is a by-product of church music. It would be difficult to improve on this statement of Dickinson:

The more generalized function of music in the sanctuary is to take possession of the prepared and chastened mood which is the antecedent of worship, to separate it from the other moods and reminiscences which are not in perfect accord with it, and to establish it in a more complete self-consciousness and a more permanent attitude. This antecedent sense of need and longing for divine communion cannot be aroused by music alone; the enjoyment of abstract musical beauty, however refined and elevating, is not worship, and a musical impression disconnected from any other cannot conduce to the spirit of prayer.

It is only when the prayerful impulse already exists as a more or less conscious tenancy of the mind, induced by a sense of love and duty, by the associations of the time and place, by the administration of the other portions of the service, or by any agencies which incline the heart of the believer in longing toward the Mercy Seat,—it is only in alliance with such an anticipatory state of mind and the causes that produce it that music fulfills its true office in public worship.[8]

Music in worship should therefore achieve the same purpose as any of the other elements of worship—the consciousness of God, the felt presence of the living Lord Jesus Christ, illumination through revealed truth, guidance by the Holy Spirit to understand and apply the revelation, the expression of love and loyalty, activating to decision, dedication, service. Music is consequently not something separate from or even supplementary to other aspects of the service of worship—it is an integral part and deserves as much preparation and consideration as any other part.

8

Enriching and Expanding
Worship

The forms of public worship tend to move from rags to riches and from riches to rags again. Elaborate, ornate worship grows cold and spiritless and is rejected. The severely plain, unadorned, poverty-stricken worship which follows gradually loses its appeal and the demand grows for something warmer, more colorful, more satisfying. A movement toward "enriching" the service arises and in the course of time worship becomes more and more elaborate until the wealth of ceremony and symbol palls on the worshipers and they seek a return to simplicity.

Is this an inevitable sequence? Is there not a middle ground which fulfils the ideal: "Give me neither poverty nor riches; feed me with the food that is needful for me" (Prov. 30:8)?

Much is being written about the recovery of liturgical worship. Thoughtful observers in churches committed to a liturgical pattern of worship frankly recognize its tendency to become stereotyped. Ceremonies that once had meaning and breathed the breath of life have in many churches become all but meaningless and dead. One has only to visit Roman Catholic churches in southern Europe and the state churches in northern Europe to observe how barren their liturgical worship has become. In North America one finds the growing movement for recovery of the vitality of the liturgy.

"Liturgy" has an unpleasant sound to many ears. The word is derived from two Greek words meaning "public" and "work" or "action." It is significant that Anglicans (Episcopalians) call their churchbook the *Book of Common Prayer*; Lutherans, *The Common Service Book*; Presbyterians, the *Book of Common Worship*; the

United Church of Canada, the *Book of Common Order*. Brenner insists that the liturgy "proclaims the right of the common man to have a part in the worship of the Christian community; to pray and not only to listen to prayer; to have part in the ceremonial and not merely to gaze upon it; to form with his own lips words of confession, of petition, of praise, of thanksgiving, of dedication and consecration."[1] Evidently there is deep-felt need to make the liturgy a living thing rather than a lifeless relic of the past.

Thoughtful pastors and people of nonliturgical churches are concerned to save their services of worship from barrenness, extemporaneousness, shallowness. They recognize that many persons of spiritual sensitivity are grieved and even shocked by the apparent disregard for propriety on the part of some congregations. They sense that there is something incongruous in noisiness, talkativeness, address to God that sometimes borders on flippancy, music that lacks quality, procedures that are unplanned and unregulated, preaching and preceding acts of worship that are unrelated, familiarity that may unwittingly breed contempt. When it is observed that worship may thus lose its true character through an overemphasis on freedom, inquiry is made as to how some of the values of liturgical worship may be obtained for nonliturgical worship.

McNutt speaks for those who are committed to free worship but who realize that it must have an appropriate framework:

Any sort of order of service will not do; the offering may not come either here, or here, or there—its place is at the moment of self-dedication; announcements, whether relevant or extraneous, are not a matter of taste merely—if they distract attention they are inexcusable. Worship leadership is a fine art—a divine art, really—and its canons cannot be violated with impunity. The religious tragedy is that so many carry on as though no such canons existed at all.[2]

Worship is not enriched merely by taking from or adding to a prescribed liturgy; neither is it enriched by amateurish liturgical imitation. An enriched service of worship will grow out of the rich spiritual experiences of those who lead and those who participate. Palmer says:

People are more apt to enter actively into the worship service of a church in which they are also engaged in doing other things actively, too. Get the members of a congregation to doing something for others under the banner of the church and they are more apt to stand at attention and even cheer when that banner is raised on any public occasion. But, if the church invites them to do nothing but worship under her auspices, the chances are they will not do even that very well.[3]

An essential of rich and satisfying worship is that it be relevant and real. Its aims should be determined by life itself. What is life doing to the people who have assembled for worship? What are their interests? their problems? their temptations? their aspirations? their failures? their achievements? their convictions? their confusions? their tensions? their satisfactions? The list may be extended as members of the congregation are passed in review.

A pastor, notable for the relevance of his preaching and the vitality of the worship he led, related that it was his custom on Wednesday night to go to the dimly lighted church auditorium, stand in the pulpit, and mentally visualize the people he expected to see in the services on Sunday. Were the songs selected suited to their interests and abilities? Would the Scriptures be vital and understandable? Would the pastoral prayer voice their communion with God? Would the offering be such as to represent for them true self-dedication? Would the sermon bring them face-to-face with Christ as Saviour and Lord? Would its conclusion and invitation lead to dedication and action? Would the total service send them away having had spiritual experiences according to the need of each which would sustain them for the week ahead? Would there be practical carry-over from this experience into the everyday affairs of life? This week-by-week review enabled him to weed out from the service irrelevances and artificialities. Worship for all present became a life-remaking experience.

Worship is enriched by the wise use of symbols. A symbol is that which represents to the senses something or someone not tangibly present. Words are our most frequently used symbols. The church house itself is symbolic of that which takes place within it. Windows may contain figures that represent religious persons, events, or truths. The communion table, with its inscription "In Remembrance of Me" reminds us of the Lord's Supper. The baptistry symbolizes death, burial, resurrection. Music represents, through poetry and melody, truths of religion and convictions and sentiments of the people. The bowed head in prayer symbolizes reverence. The attire of the minister and the choir may set them apart as leaders of worship. Giving symbolizes sacrifice. The preacher's invitation symbolizes the call to decision and action. Welcome into the fellowship of the church is often symbolized by the upraised hands of the congregation and the handclasp of Christian fellowship.

The symbols mentioned above are often scarcely recognized as such. They are symbols, nevertheless, and their meaningful use can be made to enrich the services of worship. More obvious are such symbols as the cross, candles, the crucifix, the rosary, holy oils and holy water, ashes, palms, incense, medals, the sign of the cross, the vestments of the priests and their attendants. Symbolic also are statues, paintings, and objects of veneration. The multiplication of these symbols became an offense to the Reformers, who saw in them temptations to idolatry and whose efforts to rid the churches of these "images" gave to them the name of "iconoclasts."

The break between the Eastern Church and the Western Church in the eighth century was chiefly over the use of images. Emperor Leo, III, decreed the destruction of such images but at the second Council of Nicea (787) a compromise was reached according to which the cult of images was sustained as veneration, not adoration. From time to time iconoclastic controversies raged but the iconoclasts ultimately lost. The Reformation brought about a resurgence of iconoclasm both on the continent and in England. Since that time, Protestant churches generally have rejected images.

Revulsion from the Roman Catholic abuses of symbols led some of the Reformers and Dissenters to a rejection of almost all symbolism. The house of worship must have four bare walls with a roof, and an interior wholly unadorned, with worship services so stripped of symbolism as to be barren. The effects of this swinging of the pendulum are still felt in many free church circles.

The growing desire for an enriched service of worship poses the question afresh concerning the use of symbols. How much symbolism is permissible? When do symbols become objectionable? What symbols are allowable? How can symbols be properly used without risking abuse? Categorical answers to these questions would scarcely be in order. Doctrinal convictions and denominational traditions would have to be taken into account. Social and cultural standards would also have to be considered.

The psychological aspect of the use of symbols is important. The "field" of consciousness includes a great variety of experiences. Personality wholeness or health depends largely on the integration of these experiences about a controlling center. The center may be self or God. The *self* is an objective reality; *God* is subjectively perceived. If God remains a symbol only, and does not also become reality in experience, he will be subordinated to self or will disappear from consciousness altogether.

How can the symbol take on reality? It can be objectified as image, altar, cross, candle, holy place or holy person, ritual or sacrament. The object or person or ceremony may aid the worshiper in realizing the reality of God and this ideally is the purpose of such symbols. What easily happens, however, is that the worship of the unseen God is transferred to the tangible symbol by means of which he is worshiped. The result is idolatry in fact, and to speak of it simply as "veneration" is to be unrealistic as regards the experience of the great majority. Thus "veneration" of Mary and the saints becomes worship for the many; the sacraments become means of salvation, and the church becomes a saving institution rather than an institution of the saved. The true meaning of worship is corrupted if not lost.

The same sort of thing, even though in lesser degree, may happen in evangelical circles. The church house may in and of itself become a sacred place. Attending its services and supporting its causes may be conceived of as earning merit with God. Good fortune may be expected from possessing a Bible and listening to preaching and teaching. Baptism and the Lord's Supper may be expected to bestow grace apart from the believer's faith. Worship may bring "peace of mind" and escape from reality. These misconceptions may constitute a subtle form of idolatry by taking the place of God himself and substitute for the reality of Jesus Christ and the Holy Spirit.

Ministers and congregations must, therefore, be continuously aware of both the value and the danger of symbolism. It is clear that symbols of some kind are a necessity for worship; yet it is equally evident that symbols may destroy worship. Carrol Wise puts it succinctly:

> The reality of religious symbols grows out of an intrinsic association between the experience and the form of expressions, an association grasped by insight or by faith. Insight and faith are functions of the whole personality, not of a part. The emotional and qualitative aspects of personality, as well as the intellectual, find expression in religious faith, and are always involved in the dynamic association between symbol and reality. . . . The language of religion seeks to express something that is fundamentally real in the inner life of the believer through an analogy with something that is real in his external life. . . . For the formulation of a way of life is an art involving the ability first to find meaning and then to express that meaning in living symbols.[4]

Worship is enriched by the use of art forms. Art and religion have always had an affinity. Both seek to communicate ideals and insights. The grotesque totem poles of the North American Indians and the beautiful statuary of the Greek sculptors have in common the effort to put into visible form the longing of the human spirit for idealistic expression. Art of every kind, however crude or refined, has this purpose—to communicate mental imagery through outward form. The form may be music, painting, sculpture, architecture, landscaping, writing, or any other of the varied arts. It rises above artisanry when it transcends performance and appeals to emotion as well as to intellect, when it is more concerned with truth and beauty than with utility.

The Greek philosophers recognized the inseparableness of the trilogy—truth, beauty, goodness. The Christian religion is inescapably concerned with truth and goodness. To neglect beauty is to leave a broken span in the arch. Beauty is difficult to define but easy to recognize. Beauty results when there is a combination of lines, colors, sounds, or words that is pleasing and inspiring to the beholder or listener. Ugliness is intuitively repulsive. There is something deeply significant about a religion whose devotees represent their deities by images that are ugly and repellent.

It is significant that God's revelation of himself in the Bible emphasizes the beautiful in his nature, his creation, and his worship. The Preacher looked about him and said concerning God, "He has made everything beautiful in its time" (Eccl. 3:11). The psalmist expresses the deep longing of the human heart in his craving for a place of worship where he might go "to behold the beauty of the Lord, and to inquire in his temple" (Psalm 27:4). The tragedy of Israel was that when the Messiah came, they saw in him no beauty that they should desire him (Isa. 53:2). It is the Christian's delight to sing of Jesus as "the Lily of the valley, the fairest of ten thousand."

A church that neglects art in worship is missing a divinely given opportunity. In its use of music this has long been recognized, but in the use of other art forms many churches have been negligent. Architecture is an example. The stately Gothic cathedral and the lovely Grecian chapel lacked utility. Not only so, but they were expensive. In evangelical churches, especially in America, the demand arose early for a church house that could be used for a variety of purposes, especially educational and social. In many areas, the church building must of necessity be inexpensive. Frequently in the beginning the building consisted of one room designed primarily for preaching. Those who built these utilitarian church houses usually knew nothing of architecture and felt that they did not need or could not afford the services of an architect. The result was that across the land church houses were built with little or no attention given to architectural design. Sometimes they were architectural monstrosities. It would not be true to say that people could not worship in these houses offensive to good taste. There was worship in spite of ugliness, but it would have been enhanced had more attention been given to beautification.

Pictures may be properly used to enrich worship. Paintings that represent Jesus Christ, Mary, the apostles, or other religious figures are of doubtful propriety and value in the place of public worship. Stained glass windows, once constructed with almost infinite pains and patience by specialized craftsmen, would rarely be desired in a modern church house. Such paintings as were characteristic of the Middle Ages and the Renaissance—panels, frescoes, mosaics—would scarcely be desirable or possible in the majority of today's churches. Yet artistry of high order is called for in the decoration of the house of worship, so that colors will not clash, lights will not glare, proportions will not be unsymmetrical, lines will not be out of balance.

In the worship service, use may be made of the great masterpieces of art for illustrative purposes and to induce attitudes of interest and reverence. Projected art masterpieces, available on slides and filmstrips, may be quietly and appropriately introduced at a point in the service for much the same purpose and effect as the use of music. Here is a field of opportunity for the enrichment of worship that needs much further exploration.

Poetry may serve to enrich worship. The poet is a creative artist. The very word means "one who makes or creates." The true poet does more than put into words with rhythm and rhyme thoughts that might otherwise be expressed in prose. The poet sees more deeply than others into life and its meanings and expresses his insights with rhythmic beauty. This makes what he says acceptable and memorable. The poet's skill lies largely in his use of figures of speech—comparisons that illuminate the idea and give it penetrating power. Much of the Old Testament and a considerable portion of the New Testament are in poetic form. Most of the music used in services of worship is inseparable from its words if it is to possess abiding value.

Poetry in worship can be used in more ways than to adorn a sermon. There are many collections of religious poetry from which selections may be made that communicate truth with beauty and effectiveness.[5] Printed in the bulletin, an excerpt from a great poem may be read in unison by the congregation just as they sing a song together. The recitation of a noble and inspiring poem by a good reader may occasionally take the place of the solo. The dramatic reading of such a poem may be by trained voices in concert as an anthem is sung by the choir. A verse of great poetry may be used as a call to worship, a response preceding or following the offering, or a prayer to be said by pastor and people. There is as good reason that worthy and appropriate poetry or prose excerpts should be used in worship without music as that the same thoughts should be set to music and sung.

Worship may be enriched by drama. To many earnest church-goers, "drama" means "theater" and they would immediately ask with Paul, "What partnership have righteousness and iniquity? Or what fellowship has light with darkness? What accord has Christ with Belial?" (2 Cor. 6:14-15). This association of drama with theatricals is unnecessary and unfortunate. Drama is one of the fine arts and has been closely associated with religion through the ages. Drama has a technique of its own but seeks to serve the same ends as music, painting, sculpture, literature, and other art forms. Its purpose is to present truth and to make it come alive through characters who enact a story that gives insight into life.

Much of the Old Testament is presented in dramatic form and has provided materials for some of the great dramas of modern stage and screen. The classical Greek plays were religious in character. The actors were considered ministers of religion and the amphitheaters in which the plays were produced were held as sacred temples. The plays of Aeschylus and Sophocles were not written and produced for entertainment but for serious religious purpose. They portrayed man's finitude and weakness, his struggle with fate, the inevitability of suffering and death, the favor and vengeance of the gods. Greek drama faded out before the Christian era and Christians frowned on Roman drama, which at first was in imitation of the Greek, but which came to be primarily for entertainment and was often coarse and irreverent.

Medieval drama sought to dramatize the gospel story and from this beginning developed the mystery plays, many of them taken from the Bible and dealing with God's relation to men. Imagination was freely used in the biblical stories and often the element of comedy was introduced. The stage was a wooden platform, at one end of which were the pearly gates of heaven, at the other the flaming jaws of hell. The play usually ended with the good people going through the pearly gates to heaven and the bad characters going off into the jaws of hell.

Plays with an element of comedy grew more and more popular, and while still ostensibly religious they contained a great deal of buffoonery and hilarity. The "Punch and Judy" shows are supposed to have gotten their names from Pontius Pilate and Judas Iscariot and were caricatures. In the course of time, the theater became secularized and often vulgarized and was repudiated by the Puritans. The great dramatists of the Elizabethan period did much to restore the theater to respectability but it was still looked on by pious people as profane and taboo.

Drama in America was at first a carry-over from the English stage but in the nineteenth century began to establish a character of its own. American playwrights were more concerned with the present than the past, bolder and more creative than their English cousins. Serious theater became more realistic than romantic and often sought to shock rather than to instruct or entertain. In a lighter vein, musical comedy and light opera were highly developed, frequently with emphasis on the personal glamor of the actors and the physical beauty of the actresses and show girls. For a while vaudeville was the vogue, staged wholly with a view to entertainment and amusement. The motion picture, first silent, then vocal, vastly extended the range of the drama. Television has now brought every form of dramatics into almost every home, with far-reaching cultural consequences.

Most churches have been quick to realize that they have lost their monopoly of the public's attention. No longer do they possess ascendancy as transmitters of truth or molders of opinion. Worthily they recognize that they have neither the ability nor the facility to compete with theater, movie, radio, television. Yet there is growing realization that communication of the Christian message through drama offers possibilities of supplementing preaching that must not be ignored. A religious play, it is being discovered, whether presented live or on film, can evoke an experience of worship no less than singing and preaching. The use of such a play is not just to attract a crowd nor to entertain, any more than song and sermon are so used, but "to communicate truth by means of personality for eternal ends." Fred Eastman and Louis Wilson wrote: "If a play sends an audience away exalted in spirit, with a deeper sense of fellowship with God and man, it has been religious. But if it does not have that effect it is not religious although all its characters are biblical and its story taken from the Bible itself."[6] Often there is within a church membership talented persons who could write and produce plays that would lift worship to a new level.

Worship may be enriched by pageantry. Simpler and more easily presented than the play, the pageant tells a story that is not dependent on dialogue. Pageantry takes the form of spectacle rather than discourse. Most churches are familiar with pageantry in the celebration of Christmas. The story of the birth of the Christ Child is told by means of scenes that gather about the Nativity, usually with appropriate Scripture reading and singing. The Easter story may likewise be portrayed. Pageantry may be used on historical occasions to represent biblical events, to present the missionary appeal, to promote worthy causes, to confront a congregation with human needs that call for response and action. A church pageant is not just an extravaganza for the entertainment of the congregation but is a serious effort to gain attention through the unusual to that which might otherwise be presented through the spoken word. A religious pageant may well be thought of as a visualized call to worship, accompanied by a sermon that is seen rather than heard.

All the services of worship for which a church is responsible are by no means confined to its stated meetings. Three major life crises should be surrounded by the worshipful concern of a church—marriage, birth, death.

Modern marriage is a civil contract, legalized by the state and entered into on its authority. Yet it was not always so. Religious sanctions of marriage are older than legal. The marriage ceremony among savages served a religious purpose. Roman law strictly regulated marriage and gave it religious sanction. Marriage, although not always accompanied by religious ceremony, was held sacred under Mosaic law. Early Christian marriage customs combined Jewish and Roman elements. In the Roman Catholic ecclesiastical system, marriage was made a sacrament conveying divine grace and, therefore, could not be received by an unbaptized person. The Roman Church claimed that solemnization of marriage fell within its exclusive jurisdiction. This claim was generally recognized throughout western Europe, hence clergymen were vested with authority to perform the wedding ceremony. In predominantly Protestant countries, the privilege and responsibility of performing the wedding ceremony continued to be granted to ministers of religion. By general consent, a church, through its ministerial representative, joins with the state to make the marriage contract as binding as possible.

It follows that the minister and the church are under obligation to see that everything possible is done to guarantee the permanence of the contract. An important aspect of this duty is to make the occasion worshipful. If the ceremony is performed in the church, it should in all details be conducted as reverently as any other service involving worship. The minister and church are remiss if they permit a church wedding to become an occasion of pomp and show. The ceremony performed privately, at home or in a chapel, is still the responsibility of minister and church, and should be performed only when it can be given Christian sanction and solemnized reverently.

Birth is a many-sided life crisis. The birth of a baby is an eternally significant event. A life has entered time and will continue existence through eternity. For the parents, the birth of the baby means a turning point in their lives. Never will they be quite the same again. For relatives, the community, and society as a whole, the coming of a new member of the human family is fraught with consequences. Birth is God's way of renewing the human family.

Recognition of this significance was made early by the church through the administration of baptism. In Catholic theology, this sacrament, properly administered, guaranteed the individual's ultimate salvation. When sacramental regeneration was repudiated, church practice in many evangelical circles swung to the opposite pole so that no recognition was given to the birth of children of its members. A mediating position was taken by some church groups in a ceremony of "christening" which followed the formula of baptism. In some instances, when baptism was objectionable, a service of dedication of infants was observed.

Conceding that baptism is inappropriate and that even parents have no right to dedicate the life of another, a service of recognition of newborn children within the church's membership and the self-dedication of parents to their children's Christian nurture may well have a place in the worship service. The occasion may be one of joy and thanksgiving for God's gift of the babies, heart-searching recognition by the church of its responsibility for them, and dedication of parents and relatives to the upbringing of the children "in the nurture and admonition of the Lord." The names of the new babies on the Cradle Roll may be called and their parents recognized in a deeply moving experience of worship.

Death is the irreversible life crisis. In its presence all men must stand with awe. Archaeological findings indicate that prior to recorded history some form of funeral service was performed for the dead. The intuition of immortality is as deep as life itself.

Again, minister and church should join in making the funeral a worshipful occasion. Otherwise, heathen elements may intrude into a Christian funeral service. Care should be taken to minimize or eliminate those aspects of funeral customs that make the service overemotional or too extravagant and laudatory. The purpose of the service is to treat with respect the body of the person from whom the spirit has passed and to comfort and encourage those who remain.

The spirit of worship cultivated in the church should extend to all other areas of life. As important as is public worship within the church edifice, it is no more important than worship in the home. Ministers and churches should never be satisfied with worship, no matter how satisfying and adequate, that stops short of nurturing worshiping families. In vain do we build houses of worship, train ministers and choirs to conduct worship services, perfect rich orders of worship, repeat the words of worship, and listen to sermons that seek to induce worship, if, in the end, the people go to worshipless and prayerless homes where God's presence is not felt.

Paul addressed a letter to Philemon "and the church in your house" (Philemon 2); and he sends his greetings to the brethren at Laodicea, "and to Nympha and the church in her house" (Col. 4:15). Whether Paul referred to the house of these friends as the meeting place of the church or whether he was thinking of the family or household as constituting a form of church we may not be sure. But of this we may be assured: If the church does not extend itself into the home, and if the home does not take on something of the character of the church, both home and church will ultimately fail.

There is no wealth which a church may possess nor contribution that it can make greater than that of a rich and deeply satisfying spiritual worship which extends from its services into all areas of human living.

9

Learning to Worship

Ministers and congregations, conscious of the need of more vital and satisfying worship services, may be perplexed by the problem of improvement. How shall a beginning be made? How can changes be secured without arousing resentments? May worship be taught and learned? What resources are available for worship education? Should training be for the whole congregation or for age groups? What is the educative process in teaching worship? What dangers are involved? Such questions call for practical consideration.

No matter how "free" worship may be, it will develop a pattern of some sort. Orderliness will require that the pattern be more or less regularized. Repetition results in habit and habits once formed are hard to break. We are familiar with the fact that a break in daily routine throws us out of step and creates irritation. A congregation accustomed to a given order of worship may be confused and irritated if the order is changed too radically or too often.

Granting that the present situation is unsatisfactory, how may a beginning toward improvement be made? Congregations do not like to be reminded of their bad worship habits. The over-sensitive may become angered if they are lectured or rebuked because of breaches of good form in worship. Those present for the stated church services have come to worship, not to be trained in worship.

Obviously, it is too late to do much about improvement during the course of the worship service itself. The introduction of an unfamiliar hymn for the congregation to learn to sing will distract from worship. Drilling the congregation in responsive or unison reading is an unjustifiable interference with worship. A radically new order of service, which has to be explained and practiced, mars the spirit of worship. One of the values of the prescribed liturgy is its familiarity—the people know what to expect from moment to moment. Yet this very fact may tend to make it lifeless.

There is need, therefore, for separation between corporate worship and education in worship. There is deep discernment in the division of time, according to which the educational service precedes the worship service in many churches. The hour for Bible teaching in the morning and for membership training in the evening provides occasions for teaching and training in worship that effectively prepare for participation in the experience of corporate worship that follows. The Sunday school and the Training Union (or their equivalents) have as a major function the growing of a worshiping congregation.

In the beginning of the Sunday school movement, Bible study was ungraded. The same Scripture passage was designated for all ages alike. When the educational weakness of this plan became overwhelmingly apparent, graded lessons and materials were devised. A similar development was true of the church membership training movement. As developed in America, at first it was for Young People only; then Juniors and Seniors were included; separation was then made to distinguish Juniors from Intermediates; finally, provision was made for adults and children of Nursery, Beginner, and Primary ages. Thus a well ordered church will have an adapted program of teaching and training for all age groups, with appropriate curriculum materials for teachers and pupils.

This arrangement provides ideally for worship education. From the beginning of the modern teaching and training movement, the sessions began with "opening exercises." These activities were in fact miniature worship services, although often unplanned and ineffective. They included singing, prayer, Scripture reading, announcements, and devotional comments. In a one-room building, opening and closing exercises were for all ages; with the development of multiple departments and buildings for their separate accommodation, department assembly programs were conducted for the older groups and interest-centered activities provided for the children. Thus came recognition of the need and value of graded worship as well as graded teaching and training.

Not always has this opportunity for education in worship been realized and utilized. The songs sung may be haphazardly chosen and of poor musical quality. The prayers may be by those who have made no previous preparation. The Scriptures may be irrelevant and poorly read. The announcements may be tedious and unnecessary and the "devotional" taken up with promotional talk or the reading of an "inspirational" selection. Latecomers may disturb and an atmosphere of inattention or even irreverence may prevail. It is doubtful if such "opening exercises" have really opened anything or exercised anybody!

Much thought needs to be given to the improvement of this aspect of the teaching and training program. It is now being recognized that the assembly period is as valuable for teaching purposes as the study period. Teaching and learning are greatly enhanced if preceded by a preparatory worship experience in the assembly room and followed by a consummatory corporate worship experience in the auditorium.

The assembly service gives ideal opportunity for lifting the level of music by use of the great hymns of faith and in the learning of new hymns. Opportunity is given for practice of purposeful prayer, for drill in responsive and unison Bible reading, for better understanding of the meaning and objectives of worship, for acquisition of skills in worship participation, for deepening appreciation of the privilege of worship. With themes of worship related to the Bible materials or topics to be studied, the assembly service can lead to understanding and appreciation of the well-planned and integrated service of corporate worship. Thus prepared, those who have been in the teaching and training sessions will find their enjoyment heightened and their experiences enriched as they participate in the larger worship service.

Little children can be led to sense the presence of God and to respond with reverence and love. Even the bed babies in the Nursery can be made to feel that there is something different about the place to which they go on Sunday because of the loving attention which they receive and the happiness of those who take care of them.

Beginners ask questions that lead to God as he has revealed himself in Jesus Christ and in his Book. By the age of five the normal child has acquired a vocabulary and a variety of experiences that will give reverent familiarity with activities that constitute worship. If such worship is genuine and natural, the child will gain ideas of God and of Jesus that may shape his personality for all the years to come and make more certain that, being thus led toward Christ, he will be led later to receive Christ and to become an active member of his church.

Children of Primary age are ready for deeper and more extensive experiences of worship. Unless their ideas are distorted by blundering adults, their religious concepts can be made sound and wholesome and they can be prepared for the struggle with sin and temptation that is bound to come. As important as are these years for laying sound foundations of Bible knowledge, they are even more important for worship experiences that make religion real. Nothing that Primary workers do is of more significance than their leadership of meaningful and fruitful worship.

Junior boys and girls delight in active worship participation. They grow restless when the leader becomes too dominant and their sharing is minimized. Worship for Juniors should never be thought of as passive hearing but rather as active doing. Juniors like the verse, "Be doers of the word, and not hearers only" (James 1:22) and they want to see it put into practice in their assembly worship as well as in the department and class activities.

Juniors are sensitive to their surroundings. They respond negatively to a department assembly room that is dark and cheerless, or that has cast-off pews for seats, or that lacks fresh air and cleanliness, or bears no marks of efforts to make it orderly and attractive. Juniors respond adversely to department officers and teachers who arrive late, who have not made adequate preparation, or who behave carelessly or irritably. It is no wonder that problems of "discipline" arise when the atmosphere of worship is lacking and when the example of leaders begets inattention and irreverence.

Almost any group of Juniors can be transformed from "noisy brats" to well-behaved boys and girls if sufficient care is given to preparation for worship, and then to the conduct of the total program in the spirit of worship. Stereotyped assembly programs should be avoided and much care given to arrangement of the service so as to call forth creative activity on the part of the Juniors themselves. Always it should be borne in mind that the assembly period is of high importance for the training of Juniors in worship. Thus trained they will eagerly and intelligently take part in the larger service of corporate worship which follows.

Intermediates abhor the trite and commonplace. Their dislike of dullness is evident in their reaction to assembly programs that are monotonous, repetitious, stereotyped. The designation "Intermediate" indicates that these adolescents have one foot in childhood and the other in adulthood. They are confronted with many difficult problems of adjustment. To expect too little of them and to treat them as children is fatal; to expect too much of them and treat them as adults is disappointing. Their mood is usually that of questioning and even of skepticism. Childhood religious assumptions are brought under criticism, authority once taken for granted is now questioned, inherited ideas of religion are re-examined, customary morality is met with the question, Why?

Of utmost importance to these boys and girls in this "storm-and-stress" period of life are genuine experiences of worship. Even when concealed by the veneer of sophistication, the need of God is felt and the longing for the ideal is present. Churchgoing Intermediates usually have no hesitation in expressing their interest in spiritual things and stand ready to share in worship activities. Many of them have capabilities that need only to be given opportunity. They can plan worship programs that often astonish their leaders. Given materials and encouragement, they will devote time and energy to provide good music, put on plays and pageants, develop worship themes and make constructive and original use of visual aids. Such creative experiences of worship will vitalize their Bible study, attract and hold them for the church, motivate them for wise life decisions, and prepare them for the later stage of youth with strength to resist temptation and power to make their lives count for the most. Scarcely anything that leaders of Intermediates can do will pay richer dividends than to give guidance in worship experiences.

Characteristically, youth is a period of idealism. Young people past sixteen are leaving the stage of adolescent adjustment and entering the era of achievement. Romantic dreams mingle with practical plans as marriage and career loom ahead. If the decision for Christ has not been reached and is not made during these years before full maturity, the probability of becoming Christian grows steadily less. If already Christian, young people are at a turning point as to whether their religious and church life will be wholehearted or nominal. They need more than lessons and programs and sermons—they need God. Their problems of exercising saving faith and maintaining vital Christian life will rarely find solution apart from relation to a church where they experience the transforming power of worship.

Worship for young people should possess elements of idealism, adventure, challenge. Jesus Christ, as object of worship, provides perfectly these essentials. Christianity is fortunate beyond all other religions in the appeal of its founder to youth. In him is found the supreme twofold ideal of personal fulfilment and social redemption. His call is to the highest conceivable end—the kingdom of God on earth as in heaven. His challenge is to the acceptance of a revolutionary principle—the losing of life to save it. Worship services for Young People should, therefore, gather about dynamic themes, such as Life, Faith, Love, Hope, Truth, Loyalty, Sacrifice, Purity, Happiness, Duty, Service, Patriotism, and the like.

Young people possess initiative and will enter with enthusiasm into projects that call for development of their own worship services rather than taking them ready-made from printed sources. Themes selected may be related to current Bible lessons or Training Union or youth fellowship discussions. A wealth of source materials is available in books and magazines. Life experiences as worship materials may be utilized. The Bible is an inexhaustible source of worship materials and should always be basic. Music is indispensable and should be selected for its relevance and worship value. Brevity is a cardinal virtue, since the worship period must not encroach on the teaching or discussion period. Youth groups are deprived of one of their rights and the church is made to suffer loss if worship as conceived and described above is not a part of their Christian education.

Do adults need education in worship? Notwithstanding difficulties involved, adults perhaps are in greater need at this point than younger groups. The majority of adults in many churches have suffered educational neglect in the field of worship. To them, worship may have meant sitting through a church service with directed participation as they stood and sat, listened and sang, bowed for prayer and contributed when the offering plate was passed. Their assembly periods have usually consisted of group singing, Scripture reading, prayer, brief "devotional," announcements, often with little or no relation to the Bible lesson or the group discussion. Many thoughtful adults have questioned the value of this procedure, wishing rather that the time might be given to study or discussion, but have gone along because it was customary and, apparently, necessary for promotional purposes.

Adult church groups need the energizing which comes from planned services that give rise to worship experiences. Lacking such experiences, many adults find the assembly period dull, uninteresting, profitless. No wonder they sometimes deliberately arrive late or go to their classrooms and await the termination of the "opening exercises"! With these meager ideas of worship, they then go into the service of corporate worship (if they "stay for church") with passive or even negative attitudes, expecting that the best part of the hour will be when it's over.

Revolutionary change is needed in many of these groups and nothing will effect and sustain the change more certainly than worship experiences that lead to more enriched experiences. Just as lessons and discussion programs must be planned to be satisfying, so must the assembly programs be carefully and prayerfully prepared. Again, as with young people, the secret of effectiveness lies largely in the selection of worship themes about which will be gathered song, prayer, Scripture reading, striking presentation of a central truth, all related to the lesson or discussion that follows.

Almost as important as teachers of adults are those who constitute the assembly program committee and thus develop these themes and utilize adults in presenting them. From such experiences of worship these adults will go to their classes and discussion groups with new interest and enthusiasm, and into the larger worship service with intelligence and zest that will bring transforming power to the life of the church.

We conclude that education is not *for* worship so much as it is education *in* worship. A worshiping church does not result from sermons or lectures on worship, studies of books about worship, observing ceremonies of worship, and being exhorted to attend services of worship. A worshiping church is an outgrowth of the guided educative experiences of worshiping people. Worship learnings are attendant learnings—the knowledge, attitudes, and skills which grow out of other learning experiences.

The midweek prayer meeting affords a special opportunity for worship education. Unquestionably this midweek meeting needs to be revitalized. It grew out of the realization that something was needed to bridge the gap from Sunday to Sunday and to provide opportunity for prayer without which spiritual life would grow weak and the church's witness would grow dim. In the earlier years of evangelical churches in America, the prayer meeting was taken seriously by pastor and people and was considered next in importance to the Sunday services. People of this bygone generation lived under less pressure and were more isolated; the midweek service provided a place to go for fellowship with their neighbors. In the absence of the minister, who could be present only on his appointed Sunday, often the meeting was conducted by deacons and other mature members. Conditions have vastly changed, yet many churches persist in the effort to maintain the traditional pattern of the prayer meeting.

Bernard Clausen raised the question with ministers: "Would you go to prayer-meeting if you did not have to?"[1] Candor would compel some ministers to confess that they would not. A minister told of an enforced absence from his church, during which time he turned the prayer meeting over to the deacons. Attendance dwindled until they discontinued the meeting. When the minister returned, he related, he did not reinstate the meeting. "What did your church members say about it?" someone inquired. "They never found it out!" he replied. Would most members of the typical church miss the prayer meeting if it were omitted? Clearly something needs to be done about an inherited custom if it thus falls into disuse.

John Huss decided to rename the service as "The Hour of Power." Utilizing a large number of people, making prayer and worship central, he succeeded in getting the midweek service as well attended as the Sunday services. His example, with variations, is being followed by many churches, "Family night" or "church activities night" brings the people together for a fellowship meal, group meetings according to interests and needs, followed by a period of prayer and informal worship that vitalizes all else.

"Prayer," wrote George Buttrick, "is the lost word." Further,

If prayer fails, scientific skepticism may lead us back to "chaos and old Night." If prayer stands, our nihilistic concepts of "natural law" must reel back defeated. In the key-city of prayer two irreconcilable world-views are locked in epochal strife. Perhaps the impatience of skepticism with prayer is due, not to any outmodedness in prayer, but to skepticism's own deep misgiving. . . . Religion must be quick to realize that prayer is the key-city—the real focus of man's present unrest. For prayer is the heart of religion. "Prayer is the very sword of the Saints."[2]

Prayer is not the whole of worship but it is its heartbeat and life-blood. A church praying will accomplish more than a church studying lessons, listening to sermons, taking part in ceremonies, conducting campaigns, increasing its membership and enlarging its budget. Enamored of "success," churches may forget that their power is from God and that if they lose contact with him the source of their power is gone. It may well be that the meeting for prayer, where the meaning of worship is recovered, is the most significant occasion in the life of a church.

So all-important is worship, with prayer its dynamic, that at least once a year a special season should be set apart for its consideration. Churches are accustomed to the scheduling of special occasions for evangelism, enlistment, leadership recruitment and training, stewardship, community welfare, and so on. Why not head the list with a week of worship emphasis? Groups would meet for the graded study of worship; discussions would be held concerning the meaning, value, and problems of worship; a committee would examine and evaluate the church's concepts and practice of worship; a demonstration of worship at its best could be given; books on worship and sources of worship materials could be exhibited and reviewed; superintendents of Sunday school departments and leaders of other church organizations could conduct a "clinic" in worship; the minister could preach on worship and call the church to public commitment to deeper, richer, and more regular participation in worship. Such a week would raise the standard and make more spiritually dynamic all else that the church seeks to do.

Much of the secret of success of early Methodism was in the "class meeting" of a few devout Christians who, with a leader, came together with little or no organization, seeking power from God. In many modern churches such groups are being formed, not to compete with, but to supplement the formally organized groups. An example of such a movement is the "Yokefellows," which is described as "neither a prayer group, nor a Bible study group." Its basic purpose is "to stimulate the individual to a deeper devotional life, as a result of which he comes to experience spiritual maturity, a new sense of power and peace, and an increased awareness of the manifest presence of God."[3] The concern is for sharing rather than for teaching and learning, and the quest is for deeper fellowship with one another and with God.

Such worshiping groups need not be other than those already formed in a church but may well become an essential activity of the group as it meets for the deepening of its spiritual life. An occasional prayer meeting may break up into prayer groups which will spend the hour in the sharing of needs and aspirations. They may seek to find for their lives the will of God in Christ, in praying together for objects on their hearts, and in fresh determination to go out under the guidance of the Holy Spirit to bear Christian witness and to serve human need. Such group experiences would indeed be education in worship that would yield eternal dividends.

10

Enlisting the Aid of Psychology

Worship assumes an objectively real object of worship. Isaiah's description of the workman who fashions an idol from a tree and then uses the residue for fuel to cook his meals makes idolatry senseless and ridiculous. Yet the idolator believes that the image represents reality when he worships it, praying, "Deliver me, for thou art my god!" (Cf. Isa. 44:12-17.) When the object of worship is recognized as unreal, a figment of imagination or a symbol of nonpersonal power, worship becomes psychologically impossible. There may be moments of awe and wonder but worship as a way of believing and behaving disappears.

Psychology undertakes the scientific study of human nature and conduct. Its primary source material is experience and its main methods introspection and observation. As scientists, psychologists are not concerned to affirm or deny the existence of God or the truth of Christianity or any other religious faith. As human beings, they cannot escape a certain amount of bias for or against the belief in God and the claims of revealed religion.

Worship is experience, hence is a legitimate field of psychological study. Its phenomena are observable, its effects can be introspectively reported, its outcomes can be analyzed. Since E. D. Starbuck's *The Psychology of Religion* and William James's *Varieties of Religious Experience*,[2] near the turn of the century, a wealth of literature, more or less scientific, has appeared dealing with the psychological aspects of religion. Scientifically-minded writers have sought rational explanations of worship.

Worship may be explained as placating deity. The argument runs thus: Always men have had rulers with authority over them. Kingship is an ancient institution. The monarch, invested with authority, has control over the lives of his subjects, who naturally seek to culti-vate his favor. They bow before him, they extol his virtues and sing his praises, they bring offerings to him as they make their petitions; when he is angry they seek to placate him. However, as powerful as the monarch may be, he has limitations. He cannot control the weather or floods and storms or life and death.

By analogy, there must be one with supernatural power whose control extends to all things. His favor is to be sought by bowing before him, extolling his virtues and singing his praises, bringing offerings to him when petitions are made, and placating him when he grows angry. Thus, according to this view, arises the idea of God and the practice of worship.

Another explanation of worship is sought from social psychology. Living together, men find through experience that some customs are helpful, some are hurtful; some customs are desirable, others are undesirable. To respect and care for parents, to recognize the right of private ownership, to hold life sacred, to practice chastity, to be truthful and honest are virtues proved by experience to be of greater value to the tribe than disrespect of parents, theft, murder, promis-cuity, deceit, and fraud.

How may the desirable be perpetuated and the undesirable elimi-nated? The answer is: attach religious sanctions and taboos. In Oriental culture, care of parents was insured by means of ancestor worship. In Occidental culture, the family was safeguarded by making marriage a sacrament. Observance of other essentials of the moral code was likewise associated with divine worship and violation was brought under divine disapproval. Worship is, therefore, uni-versal because of its proved pragmatic value.

Again, worship may be explained in terms of the psychological formula of stimulus and response. The human organism is capable of receiving and responding to a great variety of stimuli. These responses, repeated with satisfaction, became more or less automatic as habits. A stimulus producing a response may be associated with another stimulus so that when the original stimulus is removed the associated stimulus will produce the same response. Thus a word may evoke the same image as the object for which the word stands.

In this way behavior is successively reconditioned until ideas take the place of objects.

At first, it is pointed out, objects are worshiped and worship takes the form of activity. Then substitutions are made by words, music, ceremonials, prayers, offerings, and so on. Personal satisfactions and social approvals establish worship habits and these persist as they are handed down from generation to generation. The Gestaltists or "field" psychologists, who see experience as forming configurations or patterns, and who go from wholes to parts, admit the need of an uncreated creator who is greater than the created universe, recognition of whom constitutes worship. In this view, a place is made for worship, but the object of worship may be conceived as totality of being rather than as a divine person. Sigmund Freud, founder of the school of depth psychology, writes of religion as an illusion which springs from man's search for an integrating principle of personality. The psychiatrist or medical psychologist may or may not believe in a personal God but makes use of the concept as having therapeutic value if it aids in the recovery of mental health.

These attempts at psychological explanation of worship may result in explaining it away. The assumption may be that the reality of God is improbable but that the idea of God has certain values for human living. Reason is elevated above revelation, the latter being implicitly denied. Pressed to their logical conclusion, these theories of worship make its practice difficult, if not impossible. Left without a personal object of worship, God, man looks upward for the all-seeing eye and gazes into an empty eyesocket.

A fatal weakness of these pseudoscientific explanations of worship is that they ignore sin and its consequences. Sin, by whatever name, is a fact of experience. Sin has left its tragic mark on the human race from Cain's murder of his brother to the crimes that fill each morning's newspaper. Psychologically, sin is distinguished from sins. Sin springs from motives of fear, hate, greed, jealousy, passion, guilt, covetousness. The core of sin is self-centeredness. If what is sought in life is in the interest of self, and human interaction is thus motivated, conflict is inevitable. Men fear one another because of this threat to self-interest. They are jealous of one another and hate one another when self-interest has been violated. They covet what belongs to others and lie and steal and kill to get it in order that self-interest may be enhanced.

To gratify sensual desire and to bolster their egos, men and women become fornicators and adulterers. Sins of disposition gather about this same center of self—irritableness, quarrelsomeness, censoriousness, self-righteousness, stinginess, unforgiveness—the universal sins which "so easily beset us."

An older view of sin held that it should be dealt with by repression. Early in Christian theology, human nature was considered evil, and therefore to be despised, immolated, or at least kept under rigid control by harsh discipline. This view of the treatment of sin led in medieval times to asceticism, which in the end proved a dismal failure. The monasteries and convents into which people withdrew that they might separate themselves from the world and "crucify the flesh" became hotbeds of iniquity. Ascetic worship turns out to be self-worship.

Swinging to an opposite extreme, a school of psychology arose which held that since repression fails and is fraught with danger, unacceptable impulses and acts (sins) should be given expression. Expressing rather than repressing the hidden desire would act as "catharsis," ridding the moral organism of poisons somewhat as a cathartic rids the physical organism of toxins. In this view worship, being repressive, may actually be harmful. This "let yourself go" psychology proved even more hurtful than its ascetic opposite.

Realizing that life goes wrong and that men hurt themselves and others, a psychiatric view of sin arose. According to this view, sin is a form of mental disorder. The "sinner" has become disoriented, so that he sees himself and others in a distorted light. He can no longer make clear distinction between "mine" and "thine." His possessive instinct is exaggerated, his fears keep him continually alarmed, he sees himself unwanted and rejected, he grows hostile or depressed, he resorts to deceit or violence, and in other ways gives evidence of mental abnormality. On such a person judgment is not to be passed and punishment is of little or no avail. What the "sinner" needs is psychiatric care. If he is a juvenile, his delinquency is to be treated as a social illness for which parents and society are responsible. Viewed thus, worship may be conceded to have therapeutic value, but only because its socializing function helps to restore mental balance. A continuously rising crime rate bears witness to the fallacy of this theory of sin.

Behaviorism or psychological determinism sees man as the creature of heredity and environment. Its proponents hold that only behavior can be objectively studied—all else is subjective speculation. Behavior is predetermined by the inherited capacity of the organism for responding to unbidden stimuli. Mind and will disappear as realities, becoming convenient designations of forms of organismic behavior. Since conduct could not be other than what it is, moral responsibility vanishes and with it goes sin. Mistakes may be made but they are "falls upward" in the evolutionary process. Worship is a carry-over from the age of ignorance before science revealed the true nature of human nature as biologically and environmentally determined. The record of recent disasters, unmistakably caused by sinful human choices, has left bankrupt this behavioristic view of sin.

A religious cult, claiming to be based in "science and the Scriptures," and relying largely on unscientific formulation of psychological principles, undertakes to deal with sin by denying its existence. Its practitioners and their followers do not deny that sin, suffering, and death occur in human experience, but assert that they do not have the reality of "absolute substance or being." Sin and its consequences, it is claimed, can be banished by eliminating them from thought and recognition. Such a view has done little to rid the world of sin or diminish its disasters. Worship of a kind is maintained but more as a means to health and happiness than as honoring and serving God.

Are we to conclude that psychology, skeptical of the existence of God and without remedy for sin, has no positive contribution to make to the understanding and practice of Christian worship? On the contrary, more recent investigation has taken a turn that gives rich promise of scientific support of what the Christian, from revelation and experience, has known all along.

Turning from unsatisfying speculations concerning God, sin, and worship, thoughtful psychologists are seeking explanations in the realm of personality. Personality may not be fully explained but it cannot be explained away. Selfhood uniquely separates the human from the nonhuman and the subhuman. By its very definition, selfhood involves self-determination. Persons may be activated by self-interest or they may sacrifice self-interest for the sake of others. In the presence of the lower, they may choose the higher. Rather than bowing to a monarch, seeking to placate him and so to gain favor, men may defiantly rebel and give their lives in the cause of freedom.

Instead of conforming to established religious sanctions and taboos, men may revolt and go contrary to custom, regardless of the cost. Instead of responding like robots to situations of stimulation, men may determine to change conditions; or if they cannot change them, to respond in opposite ways, stubbornly refusing to obey the "laws" of behavioristic determinism. Finding themselves under pressure to adjust to a world pattern, men may resolve not to be "conformed to this world." Tempted to use religion as an escape from reality, men may find in Christ and the worship of God courage to fight the good fight, to finish the race, to keep the faith. Losing their lives, they discover that they save them.

Worship thus becomes the practical expression of Christian existentialism. Worship is not apart from understanding but it surpasses understanding. The worshiper does not need to "prove" God—he has experienced him and this experience has transformed and continues to transform his personality. The worshiper has not abandoned science, common sense, and logic; but he has discovered in himself other faculties than reason and claims the right to enrich and fulfil personality through feeling, intuition, conscience, reverence, adoration, faith, hope, love. Through reason he grasps truth but in revelation he is grasped by truth. With self at the center, the concentric circles of life turn inward and narrow to a point. With God at the center, the concentric circles turn outward and reach into the infinite.

Ceasing to be consumed with concern for the temporal only, the Christian finds himself freed from the enslavement of self and things with their "bondage to decay," and to have obtained "the glorious liberty of the children of God" (Rom. 8:21). Such experience with such results is not escapism, wishful thinking, fantasy, or glorified custom; it is demonstrable reality. The formula is not essentially different from that in the scientific field: assumption, experimentation, verifiable results. In worship God is assumed, the assumption is tried out, the results in personality are verifiable.

This psychological approach to worship and sin throws light on their relationship. The basic New Testament Greek word translated *sin* means "missing the mark." What mark? The goal of the "fulness of life" which Jesus said he came to make possible—the realization of personality potential inherent through original creation in the image of God but blocked by sin. Any realistic view of human nature and experience must face this sin blockage. What is to be done with sin if it is not to be ignored, expressed, or denied? The Christian answer is definite: Sin can be admitted, repented, confessed, lifted up to God, and forgiven. This is what happens in an experience of true Christian worship. Selfhood is not denied and self-determination is not surrendered but self-centeredness and its accompanying selfish behavior are replaced by devotion to God as revealed in Jesus Christ and to others for his sake.

Emancipation from sin is not achieved instantly; the struggle continues. Paul's experience was that of the worshiping Christian: "I do not do the good I want, but the evil I do not want is what I do. . . . For I delight in the law of God, in my inmost self, but I see in my members another law at war with the law of my mind and making me captive to the law of sin which dwells in my members." Is the situation then desperate? Paul exclaimed, "Wretched man that I am! Who will deliver me from this body of death?" Then came the answer of the worshiping Christian: "Thanks be to God through Jesus Christ our Lord!" (Rom. 7:19-25).

Personality cannot find fulfilment in isolation. In the Eden story, Adam had everything he needed except human companionship. God said, "It is not good that the man should be alone"; hence Eve was given to him that in each other they might find completeness. Together they experienced sin, suffering, parenthood, retribution, fulfilment of their destiny.

It is neither good for man to live alone nor possible. Living wholly apart from other persons, one would be less and other than a person. Wardens know that the severest punishment for a prisoner is solitary confinement. Husbands and wives know that the cruelest retaliation is withdrawal from each other. Parents suffer most when a wall of separation is built between them and their children. Community spirit dies when neighbors are divided and nations decline to extinction when they become isolated.

Psychological isolation is a far greater barrier to community than physical boundaries. The invisible "Iron Curtain" of Russia shuts her off from the free world far more effectually than did the "great wall" of China. With physical barriers almost eliminated by rapid transit and communication, people today are separated as never before by psychological barriers. Invisible walls are built that divide neighbors from neighbors; the privileged from the less privileged; employers from employees; the white race from the colored; the adherents of one political party from others; the members of one religious body from their fellows. The resultant tensions bring about "cold war" which at intervals flares into dramatic destructiveness.

Man's divisions, accounting for much human misery, go back to a prior cause—alienation from God. Let reconciliation take place on this vertical plane and peace will follow on the horizontal plane. Paul wrote with deep psychological insight concerning the restoration to fellowship of Jews and Gentiles through the blood of Christ:

For he is our peace, who has made us both one, and has broken down the dividing wall of hostility, by abolishing in his flesh the law of commandments and ordinances, that he might create in himself one new man in place of the two, so making peace, and might reconcile us both to God in one body through the cross, thereby bringing the hostility to an end (Eph. 2:14-16).

As conflict arises from lack of bonds of fellowship or from broken bonds, so fellowship is created or restored where there is a sufficiently strong bond. "Religion" is not enough; some of the most disastrous conflicts of history have arisen over religion. Worship centered in Christ provides the reconciling experience that brings peace.

Psychology has been found increasingly valuable in problem-solving. For centuries logic was the chief method used in seeking solutions to problems. A universal truth was stated, either positively or negatively, and from this major premise minor premises were inferred until a valid conclusion was reached. Such reasoning took the form known as the syllogism: all A is B; all C is A; therefore all C is B. Logical reasoning took little or no account of experience; hence, conclusions were sometimes reached that were fantastically unreal. Many of the doctrines of the Roman Catholic Church were established in this way.

While logic still has a place, it has been largely superseded by inductive or scientific problem-solving. The scientific approach reverses the logical in that it proceeds from the particular to the general. Particular facts are gathered, tested, co-ordinated, systematized, tried out under controlled conditions, then generalized as laws. The almost universal modern use of this method of problem-solving has produced the marvels of the so-called scientific age.

The scientific method of inquiry alone is as inadequate as the older method of formal logic in finding answers to problems of the human spirit. Here insight is needed and takes priority over logical reasoning or methodical research. By insight is meant perception of relationships that does not depend on syllogism or laboratory techniques. Truth by insight is not deduced from generalizations nor discovered from experimentation, though not necessarily apart from both. Such insight was often the beginning point of the philosopher and frequently accounts for the original discovery of the scientist.

The biblical prophets combined research with revelation. Inspiration is insight arising from the divine initiative. In everyday affairs, insight is often needed more than logic or science. Many of life's perplexing problems would find their happy solution if perplexed men and women possessed deeper insights. Worship is not just a method of problem-solving but provides conditions which effectually aid in finding answers to life questions.

There is a principle known as "reversed effort"—relaxation results in more fruitful thinking than strained attention. The principle is illustrated in the futile attempt to recall a name which is suddenly remembered after the effort has ceased. Always there are two aspects of mental activity—the conscious and the unconscious. An unsolved problem held long in the focus of attention creates tension and exhaustion. Strain and fatigue removed, the unconscious can often accomplish what conscious effort failed to do.

The psychological study of worship discloses its value in the solution of problems. Worship, with its focus on God, relieves the mind of futile anxiety and permits its relaxed activity on the unconscious level. This result does not require that the problem be dealt with directly by the sermon or other aspect of the worship service. A woman expressed her gratitude to the preacher for the help she received in reaching a difficult decision. "What did I say that helped you?" the minister inquired. "Nothing specifically," she said, "I just sat quietly in the presence of God for the hour and came away with my mind made up."

More directly, worship aids in problem-solving through the insights that come from wisdom and guidance higher than human efforts. Isaiah represents God as inviting him who is athirst to come to a spiritual fountain and him who is spending his money to no purpose to come to a satisfying feast "without money and without price." God thus sought is near at hand and will abundantly pardon the repentant worshiper.

> For my thoughts are not your thoughts,
>   neither are your ways my ways,
>   says the Lord.
> For as the heavens are higher than the
>   earth,
>   so are my ways higher than your ways
>   and my thoughts than your thoughts
>   (Isa. 55:8-9).

A new frame of reference for problem-solving is provided in worship. Another way than the human is discovered—the way of God as revealed in Christ and made known in the experience of worship. It may not be claimed that worship solves all problems but it can be confidently asserted that without worship multitudes bear burdens from which they might find release through worship.

Worship and psychology have much in common in their interpretation and mitigation of anxiety. Anxiety is distinguished from fear in that fear is mental distress occasioned by immediate danger; anxiety is mental distress occasioned by anticipated danger. In fear, the threat is present and recognized; in anxiety, the threat is future and less well-defined. Fear reaches its climax and runs its course; anxiety is a persistent state. Fear is often a protective reaction and when thus experienced is wholesome, even necessary to survival. Anxiety, if long continued, disorganizes personality and destroys happiness.

Anxiety is acquired, not innate. It has many expressions but limited sources. A chief source of anxiety is the feeling of inadequacy or helplessness in the face of anticipated danger, whether to the body or to personality. Early childhood frustrations, overprotection or lovelessness, continual warnings or neglected guidance, lack of praise or too much blame, overconfidence or paralyzing doubt, or other such frustrating experiences may have led to the conclusion that life is too full of risks to be enjoyed. Anxiety builds up in proportion to the sense of inadequacy in meeting demands and dangers.

The anxiety-ridden person obviously needs strengthened confidence—confidence in self, in others, in the universe as friendly, supremely in God. In worship there is tacit admission of dependence but conscious affirmation of faith in a God of providence on whom one can depend. Of such reliance Jesus spoke when he said:

Do not be anxious about your life, what you shall eat or what you shall drink, nor about your body, what you shall put on. . . . Therefore do not be anxious, saying, 'What shall we eat?' or 'What shall we drink?' or 'What shall we wear?' For the Gentiles seek all these things; and your heavenly Father knows that you need them all. But seek first his kingdom and his righteousness, and all these things shall be yours as well (Matt. 6:25-33).

Public worship provides in one of its finest forms the "therapeutic community," recognized by psychiatrists as essential to the recovery and maintenance of mental health. No one knows how much "nervous breakdown" is prevented by the prophylaxis of worship experiences. In the company of worshipers, the *I-Thou* relationship is established. Persons cease to be thought of as means to ends and become ends in themselves. Wayne Oates described this kind of spiritual communion as "fellowship based upon loving and caring, personalizing and understanding." In the *I-it* relationship

persons are objectified, and the element of communion and interpersonal love is replaced by detachment and distrust. Middle walls of partition occur in this latter instance along the lines of the defective kinds of religious attitudes. . . . This pattern of the relatedness of love leads to the supremely worthful kind of religious experience of which the Apostle Paul speaks when he says that the objectified rituals of life avail nothing, "but faith working through love" accomplishes all things. Bringing life into conformity to this kind of love and faith makes the life an "appropriate one," integrated in faith and knowledge of the "Son of God, unto a full-grown man, unto the measure of the stature of the fullness of Christ."[3]

In the main, the psychologist and the religionist have come to count each other as allies rather than as antagonists. Studying the patient's needs and seeking his restoration to health, the psychiatrist recognizes the therapeutic value of worship. Seeking to supply his parishioner's needs, the minister finds guidance from the understanding of persons supplied by the psychologist. Russell J. Becker thus stated it:

When the psychologist takes his methods of empirical investigation (be they questionnaire, experimental situation, epidemiological survey, participant observation, or whatever) to the data of religious life, the result is a welcome increase in the body of human knowledge. . . . Both the psychologist and the informed religious person have felt satisfied with the growth of a psychology of religion. To the psychologist it is an extension of a science of psychology. To the informed religious person it is an increase in our knowledge of the truth.[4]

11

Linking Worship with Evangelism

Can a worshiping church at the same time be an evangelistic church? Are the two ideals contrary or complementary? A casual observer might conclude that churches concerned for an orderly, well-planned, enriched service of worship are not usually evangelistic; while churches which are effectively evangelistic place chief emphasis on spontaneous prayer, testimony, and singing. The conclusion might be that a church must take its choice—worship or evangelism.

Such an alternative would rob the church of one or the other of its two main reasons for existence. Clearly a church has failed with respect to its primary objectives if it does not seek with all its mind to bring people into the presence of God and with all its heart to lead them to Christ. Worship with no evangelistic purpose is untrue to the New Testament concept; and evangelism that ignores worship will almost certainly be faulty and disappointing.

The psalmist sets worship and evangelism in their true relationship. David, whose sin had found him out, bowed before God in contrite and repentant worship, praying,

> Create in me a clean heart, O God,
>   and put a new and right spirit within me.
> Cast me not away from thy presence,
>   and take not thy holy Spirit from me.
> Restore to me the joy of thy salvation,
>   and uphold me with a willing spirit
>   (Psalm 51:10-12).

What will then follow this experience of worship after confessed sin has been forgiven? David says,

> Then I will teach transgressors thy ways,
>   and sinners will return to thee.
> . . . .
> O Lord, open thou my lips,
>   and my mouth shall show forth thy praise.
> For thou hast no delight in sacrifice;
>   were I to give a burnt offering,
>   thou wouldst not be pleased (vv. 13-16).

This is normative. The saved sinner through repentance gets right with God in an experience of worship; then, forgiven and cleansed, the renewed child of God bears his winning witness to the lost.

How does worship vitalize and fulfil the evangelistic work of a church? Few matters in a church's life are of greater importance than the maintaining of an inseparable relationship between these two major functions—worship and evangelism. They are like breathing and heartbeat; nerve stimulus and muscle response; light and sight; sound and hearing—the one is essential to the other. Lest worship be mistakenly thought of as unnecessary or inimical to evangelism, let us re-examine some of the particulars of the relationship.

Worship attracts lost people to the church services. The preacher as evangelist finds himself thwarted by the absence of those to whom he would make his appeal. It is not enough for him to console himself with the thought that he is to feed the sheep. His heart yearns, as did that of his Master, for the lost sheep that must be brought into the fold. Sunday after Sunday to preach the good news of Christ's salvation to those who are already saved and to appeal for decision and confession to those who have already decided and confessed is "Heartbreak Hill" for the evangelistic preacher. He realizes that his preaching alone is not enough to bring the unsaved to the church services. He therefore feels the need of a drawing power beyond himself and his message—the power of the felt presence of God in Christ as people come together for worship. "Oh, come, let us worship and bow down, let us kneel before the Lord, our Maker!" is the compelling invitation, even more than, "Oh, come, let us hear the preacher!"

A church deals unfairly with its minister when it expects him to be the "drawing card" to attract the unsaved to its services. The minister assumes a burden too heavy to bear if he accepts responsibility for the salvation of the lost through his unaided preaching. For a limited time an evangelist may draw a crowd, but a church that seeks to sustain evangelism perennially must do so through worship that is rich and warm and satisfying.

Worship purges the church of its sinfulness. One of the most startling events in the Gospel narrative is the cleansing of the Temple by Jesus. Matthew places it immediately after the triumphal entry, when Jesus rode into Jerusalem as a king and the crowds followed him shouting, "Hosanna to the son of David! Blessed be he who comes in the name of the Lord! Hosanna in the highest!" (Matt. 21:9). Then "Jesus entered the temple of God and drove out all who sold and bought in the temple, and he overturned the tables of the moneychangers and the seats of those who sold pigeons." With fierce moral indignation he declared, "It is written, 'My house shall be called a house of prayer; but you make it a den of robbers" (vv. 12-13).

The church at Corinth weakened its witness because it harbored sin in its membership—quarreling among the brethren, immorality that would have shamed the pagan, disorderly worship and contentiousness. "Cleanse out the old leaven that you may be fresh dough!" Paul exhorts (1 Cor. 5:7). What will be the consequences of "speaking with tongues" and disorderly worship? The "outsider" will be confused and conclude that these hysterical worshipers have lost their minds; but if worship is orderly and those who speak do so intelligently, the unbeliever will be convicted, he will be called to account, the secrets of his heart will be disclosed; and so, "falling on his face, he will worship God and declare that God is really among you" (1 Cor. 14:24-25).

Preachers seeking to lead in an evangelistic effort can bear witness with Paul to the stumbling block in the way of the lost because of sin and disorder in the church. A minister tells of such a situation where he sought to preach in a revival but wholly without result because of division and hostilities among the members. At midweek of the meetings he appeared before the cold congregation with Bible in one hand and his suitcase in the other. Lovingly, but bravely, he told his astonished hearers that he was leaving to catch the next train to return home; that to continue would be to wrong them and himself and to dishonor God. He pointed out that in such a cold and worshipless church it would be futile to expect the Holy Spirit to bring souls to birth. When the spirit of worship and fellowship had been restored, he said, he would be glad to come back and complete the meetings if the church so desired. With a brief prayer that they might repent and amend, he left the shocked congregation.

The preacher's courage and frankness brought results. The church underwent a spiritual housecleaning, and having restored worship and fellowship, invited the evangelist to return. In the changed atmosphere, his preaching was with power and many were won to Christ.

Worship warms the hearts of the saved. Coldness in the pew extends its chill to the pulpit, as every minister knows. Billy Sunday, the colorful evangelist of a half-century ago, expressed it trenchantly, if a bit inelegantly, when he said: "The trouble with a lot of churches is that they put the evangelist in the refrigerator and expect him to sweat!" Formal worship that is "icily regular" generates no warmth of spirit; unplanned worship that is noisily irregular develops no depth of spirit. In either case, evangelism is seriously handicapped.

Evangelism appeals to thought but not apart from feeling. The great decisions of life are not made by logic alone. Indeed, feeling often controls more than thinking in decisive moments. The supreme decision is made when a sinner turns from self and sin to Christ and righteousness, surrenders life to God, and asks for membership in the family of the redeemed. Such a shift of life center may be made in solitariness, but not often. It needs the encouragement of a company of believers, who themselves have had the experience and are deeply and warmly concerned that the unbeliever may take the fateful step.

Such warmhearted, prayerful concern, permeating a congregation, is of the very essence of worship and vitally reinforces evangelism.

Why do so few church members bear Christian testimony to their unsaved friends and acquaintances? They know Christ and have experienced his saving power. Many of them have studied the Bible in Sunday school classes for years and have sufficient understanding of the way of salvation to communicate it to others. They have long listened to gospel preaching with its simple appeal to repentance, faith, confession. Yet they go day after day, month after month, year after year, ignoring Christ's last and supreme commission, "You shall be my witnesses."

The reasons for this neglect may be varied, but is not the basic reason to be found in the lack of warmth of love for Christ and in the dearth of compassionate concern for those who do not know him and his salvation? Unless such love and compassion are aroused and maintained, no amount of teaching and preaching concerning "the plan of salvation" will turn the coldhearted Christian into an effective witness.

What will bring about the change? The answer is found in the week-by-week experience of worship. This means more than just attending church services and sitting as a spectator and listening as an auditor. It requires experiencing anew awareness of the presence of God as Father; of the reality of Christ as Saviour and Lord; of the indwelling power of the Holy Spirit; with resultant humility, confession, forgiveness, thanksgiving, and rededication. When worship is thus experienced, sharing Christ, the source of the experience, becomes natural and necessary.

Worship gives motive to witnessing. A preacher may say, "I just am not an evangelist. I preach to feed the sheep but I depend upon parents and Sunday school teachers to nurture the lambs and bring them to the time when they quietly and normally come into the adult fold."

Several difficulties make this position untenable. Preaching that has as its main purpose the feeding of the sheep will quite likely result in overfeeding with consequent obesity and inertia. Healthy sheep need more than feeding—they need exercise.

Another difficulty arises from modern population mobility. The sheep today do not stay long in one pasture! In a very real sense, church members like sheep go astray. They are like the multitude upon whom Jesus looked with compassion "because they were harassed and helpless, like sheep without a shepherd" (Matt. 9:36). The masses of adult unbelievers, moving from country to town to city and back again, must be reached for Christ and brought into his fold before they can be fed.

A fatal fallacy is involved in the expectation that parents and teachers will so nurture the children that they will of course gradually mature in knowledge and faith and thus naturally take their places as members of the adult church fellowship.

This assumption overlooks two tragic facts: The child, born of sinful parents in a sinful environment, comes early to experience the sin that separates from God, and needs a Saviour whom he must trust in a personal act of commitment. Parents and teachers should lead the child toward and to Christ but they cannot make the decision for the child to follow Christ. The other insuperable difficulty in the way of this assumption is that many parents cannot be depended on to provide Christian nurture for their children and an ever-increasing number of children are never enrolled in the school of the church. Granting that Sunday school teachers will evangelize their pupils (which cannot be uniformly taken for granted), there are unreached millions whom they will never teach.

When worship fails, either from nonattendance or from spiritual powerlessness, evangelism fails. Worship provides the motivation to seek the saving of the lost. Worship arouses the sense of urgency that brings obedience to the command, "Go out to the highways and hedges, and compel people to come in, that my house may be filled" (Luke 14:23). Worship makes vividly clear the gulf that yawns between the holy God and sinful men and deepens the desire to bridge that gulf through acceptance of the atoning work of Christ. Worship brings realization of the contamination by sin and the absolute necessity of trusting life to a loving Saviour and Lord if it is to be kept from sin's inevitable ruin.

When these considerations have laid hold on preacher and people, they are strongly motivated, as they worship together, to make the objective of their worship not just their own cultivation and enjoyment. Thus they realize that worship is a means to an end and that the end is the sharing with others the good news of God. Without such motivation, worship becomes empty—and eventually so will the church!

Worship lends power to preaching. Every preacher knows and dreads the ordeal of speaking prepared words to an unprepared audience. His frustration is illustrated by the television commercial which pictured a man firing a revolver without effect because of an "invisible shield" that stopped the bullet. The preacher delivers the message intended to reach and move his hearers, yet they seem to be insulated from him and he from them. Grateful to the clock that tells him it is time to quit, the preacher pronounces the benediction, the people file out, and he goes home with a sense of failure. The unmoved congregation senses the emptiness of it all, though mercifully they may refrain from saying so.

What accounts for this failure of the speaker to make responsive contact with his audience? A number of factors may be present. The sermon subject may lack relevance; its content may be out of the interest range of the listeners; the preacher's heart may not really be in it; distractions without or within may divert attention. Yet more than all these hindrances may be the tragic fact that God is not in the service.

A child was being scolded by his mother for his misconduct at church. "But what I did would not have been wrong anywhere else," the lad protested. "Why was it wrong at church?" Impressively his mother replied, "Because you were in God's house." Unconvinced, he retorted, "Then why doesn't God come sometimes?"

Did not the child's insight penetrate to the heart of the matter? Here is a man standing before a group of people talking to and about God but there is the feeling that God himself is not there! At the close of the sermon, the invitation is given to receive and publicly profess an absentee Christ! The whole procedure lacks reality and no one more than the preacher is conscious of the lack of power. Preaching that brings the response of conviction and conversion must be in an atmosphere of worship where the Holy Spirit takes the sermon and sends it as a swift arrow to the hearts of unbelievers. Jesus pointed to this truth when he commanded the disciples, just before his ascension, to wait until the Holy Spirit came upon them before going out to witness. The wisdom of this waiting in worship was evidenced on the day of Pentecost. The disciples witnessed and Peter preached with such power that three thousand souls were converted.

Worship produces conviction of sin. Callousness concerning sin makes modern man almost impervious to the call to repentance. The good news must be proclaimed against the dark background of the bad news of sin. Repentance is the sinner's first step toward reconciliation with God and if this step is missed there is no other. Sin, laid bare, is ugly and repugnant; however, it has been so glamorized that it is seen not as repulsive but attractive and desirable. How can sin's mask be torn away and its true nature disclosed? Jonathan Edwards made men turn from sin in horror, as he pictured "sinners in the hands of an angry God." Would preaching bring the same reaction today? With the same end in view, what approach will be effectual?

Worship has been described as "the celebration of life." Sin brings death—Christ brings life. Worshipers in effect are saying, "If we have died with Christ, we believe that we shall also live with him" (Rom. 6:8). Dead to sin—alive to God in Christ Jesus! Does not the better self in every man long to join in such a celebration? How can he be freed from the sin that prevents entrance into this new life? The slave to sin knows that he cannot free himself. He looks about him to see men like himself who are gratefully saying as they worship: "Thanks be to God, through Jesus Christ our Lord! . . . There is therefore now no condemnation for those who are in Christ Jesus" (Rom. 7:25 to 8:1). Accepting Christ's offer of this new life on the simple conditions of repentance and faith, the convinced believer steps out on the invitation of the preacher, extended on behalf of the church, makes known his experience and commitment, and is received by baptism into the fellowship of the saved. The events might have taken place apart from a worshiping congregation, but the presence of others, themselves "sinners saved by grace," is normative in bringing to conviction of sin and to conversion and action.

Worship makes public commitment fitting and normal. A worship service with evangelism as its objective should cultivate awareness of the presence of him whose preaching reached a climax in the invitation, "Come to me, all who labor and are heavy-laden, and I will give you rest. Take my yoke upon you, and learn from me; for I am gentle and lowly in heart, and you will find rest for your souls. For my yoke is easy, and my burden is light" (Matt. 11: 28-30). If worship is response to God, what could be a more fitting conclusion to a service of worship than the response of a sin-burdened soul to the call of the Saviour to come to him in repentance and faith for relief and new life?

There are some who question the propriety of thus closing a worship service. They seem to see something incongruous in the invitation given by the minister on behalf of the church to public confession of sin and profession of faith. The objection may have some validity if the climax of the service is reached in clamorous urgency that drowns out the voice of the Spirit in the effort to overcome resistance and compel unwilling response. The conditions of worship may be violated if coercive strategems are employed for the sake of securing "joiners," with little apparent concern for the genuineness of a true conversion experience and with careless respect for the inner citadel of personality. Responses made in such circumstances may by God's grace represent a saving experience, but the risk is run that they represent emotional yielding to high pressure stimulation and will not stand the test of time.

When, however, the moment of decision and action comes in an atmosphere of hushed reverence, the minister pleading on behalf of Christ "be reconciled to God," the choir reinforcing the appeal as they sing the invitation, and the praying congregation joins in the song, the experience of worship reaches its height when someone steps forward to say, quite simply and naturally, "I believe. . . . What is to prevent my being baptized?"

Is there not a serious misconception of worship that would make it a privilege of the saved, and of evangelism that would direct its message exclusively to the unsaved? God takes initiative in seeking the lost. Peter said to Cornelius, the pious but unsaved Roman officer, "Truly I perceive that God shows no partiality, but in every nation any one who fears him and does what is right is acceptable to him" (Acts 10:34-35). Peter then preached the gospel to those who accompanied him, as well as to those of the household of Cornelius, in response to which Cornelius and others believed and made it publicly known. The witness of the Holy Spirit confirmed Peter's witness, "He commanded them to be baptized in the name of Jesus Christ" (v. 48).

What could have been more natural and fitting than this outcome of a moving experience of worship? To the transformation of Cornelius and his associates must be added the change which took place in Peter and his associates. Cornelius and his group became Christians and Peter and his companions became better Christians. Should not this be the normal and expected outcome when God is worshiped, the gospel is preached, the invitation to decision and action is given, and response is publicly made?

Worship assimilates the saved into the fellowship of the church. Salvation is the end of worship—but it is the front end! Beyond the saving experience lies a lifetime of growth and service. It is tragic when the newborn Christian remains a spiritual infant. When a church receives a new member, it implicitly commits itself to that new member's continuous nurture. The analogy is that of the child born into a family—father, mother, and older sisters and brothers are under inescapable obligation for the new member's health and growth and assimilation into the life of the family.

The reception of a new member following baptism is a significant act of worship. The church worships as it authorizes administration of the rite of baptism. This authorization should not be given lightly or hurriedly but should be an expression of the congregation's awareness of the Holy Spirit's presence and power in leading to the decision and action of the applicant for membership. If worship is celebration, what may a congregation celebrate more joyously than when the gospel has done its work in the lives of those who have heard and responded, "to open their eyes, that they may turn from darkness to light and from the power of Satan to God, that they may receive forgiveness of sins and a place among those who are sanctified by faith" (Acts 26:18)?

The rite of baptism is itself an act of worship but should not be considered completed until those baptized are publicly welcomed into the household of faith by the older members. Such public recognition may well be on the occasion of the observance of the Lord's Supper, of which the newly baptized will be partaking for the first time. This meaningful ceremonial will be made all the more worshipful if appropriate recognition is given to those who have recently become members of the body of Christ, his church, who are now included in the Memorial Supper.

In a service of public worship, confession will have been made that led to church membership. In services of worship, fulfilment of this initial commitment will be found through faithful participation. The manner in which new members are received into the fellowship of the church may largely determine the relationship in the years ahead. A worshipful service of reception and recognition of new members is an obligation which no church should neglect.

Worship conserves the fruits of evangelism. Jesus said, "I chose you and appointed you that you should go and bear fruit and that your fruit should abide" (John 15:16). The sad fact is that much of the fruit of evangelism does not abide. Whatever the pastor-evangelist's theology of "perseverance" may be, he is bound to admit that too many of those who responded to the invitation and were baptized have been lost to usefulness. They may have moved away and thought so little of their church membership as never to have transferred it; or they may still be living within reach of the church but have become so indifferent that they rarely if ever attend its services, give to its support, or bear Christian witness. It is not unusual to discover that one third or even more of the membership of a church is represented by those whose fruit does not abide.

Causes of such indifference and inactivity on the part of professing Christians are often complex, but for the majority the defection begins with neglect of worship. Failure to join with others in the services of corporate worship produces spiritual deficiency. An anemic condition almost invariably results. There is loss of appetite for spiritual things. Lack of energy induces apathy, failing interest reduces Christian service. The void thus created begins to be filled by other interests and activities. Absorption in other things unrelated to the church and its purposes crowds out church attendance, continued absence from the services of worship intensifies the anemia—and so the vicious cycle continues until spiritual life all but reaches the vanishing point.

The physician knows that the stage may be reached physically which is described as "pernicious anemia," endangering life itself. He knows that radical treatment is needed, perhaps involving massive doses of appropriate vitamins, followed by blood transfusions or diet and treatment that will maintain the needed vitality. The physician of souls—the pastor-evangelist—knows that the spiritual life history of many church members follows an analogous pattern. He knows that the condition might have been prevented had the spiritually ill person maintained a balanced diet of worship and service; and he knows that recovery depends on restoring this balance.

Jesus used the unforgettable figure of the vine and the branches to show the absolute necessity of vital union with him if fruit is to be borne. Plainly he declared, "If a man does not abide in me, he is cast forth as a branch and withers; and the branches are gathered, thrown into the fire and burned" (John 15:6). That this vital union with him includes fellowship with others in worship and service is indicated by the words that immediately follow: "This is my commandment, that you love one another as I have loved you. Greater love has no man than this, that a man lay down his life for his friends. You are my friends if you do what I command you" (vv. 12-14).

In worshiping together, Christians show their love for one another as well as for Christ. In worshiping, they develop bonds of friendship that cause them to give their lives for one another. Thus it becomes possible for them to obey Christ's great commandment, that they love one another as he has loved them. In such an atmosphere of love and sacrifice, the worshiping Christian becomes the sound tree that cannot bear evil fruit. The ultimate judgment "you will know them by their fruits" (Matt. 7:16) will be passed on all alike.

There are many fruits which Christians, covenanting together in the fellowship of a church, should bear, but the most precious is the fruit of evangelism. The supreme purpose of their salvation and organization is that they may share with Christ and with one another in the saving of lost persons who will then be the saving salt in a decaying society. Such an undertaking is wholly beyond human power and resources except as these are energized by the power of God in Christ, channeled by the Holy Spirit and released among men through worship. A church at worship will be an evangelizing church.

12

Evaluating Worship

Application of the principles of testing and measuring accounts largely for the marvels of the scientific age. Crude inventions, such as the first steam engine, the original telephone, the primitive automobile and airplane, the "wireless" preceding radio and television, have been brought to their present point of perfection by measuring and remeasuring, testing and retesting, in the never-ceasing quest for improvement.

Can this principle of measuring and testing be applied to worship? Certainly the precise instruments of the physical laboratory cannot be employed in the field of intangibles of which worship is representative. The same problem is confronted that faced investigators in the beginning of the movement to test intelligence. Skeptics agreed that superior and inferior intelligence could be recognized but doubted the possibility of exact measurement, since intelligence is intangible. Yet instruments were devised according to which degrees of intelligence could be located on an accurate scale.

Attitudes, skills, choices, socialization, and similar "intangibles" can be measured today. There is, therefore, good reason to believe that worship, one of the oldest and most universal of human activities, can be measured and tested, provided adequate instruments are devised. Since we have no absolute standards of measurement, as in the physical sciences, perhaps evaluation is a more satisfactory term than measurement.

Obviously, the externals of worship can be evaluated with considerable accuracy. The location of the building, its accessibility and outward attractiveness; its freedom from undue distractions; its comfortable seating, lighting, heating; its pulpit and choir arrangements; its musical instrument or instruments; the symmetrical shape, size, and acoustics of the auditorium, and other such physical factors can be adjudged favorable or unfavorable for worship. On a scale of zero to ten, each of these and other externals may be rated—zero representing wholly unsatisfactory, ten representing fully satisfactory—the rating moving downward or upward from the median as the facts warrant.

The leadership of worship is amenable to evaluation. The minister and his associates, especially the minister of music and the instrumentalist, may be rated with a fair degree of objectivity. The rating may be on such points as (1) preparedness, (2) confidence, (3) simplicity, (4) dignity, (5) self-effacement, (6) clarity, (7) naturalness, (8) considerateness, (9) co-operativeness, and (10) reverence.

Ushers and congregation may be brought under consideration. Their behavior may determine the success of the worship service even more than that of those who lead from the platform. Observation may be concentrated on the ushers as to organization, friendliness, tactfulness, dependability; on the congregation as to quiet entrance, orderly seating, personal and group responsibility, courtesy and considerateness, and avoidance of distractions.

The congregation's sense of the importance of the services of public worship may be estimated. It should not be difficult to rate the attitudes and habits of the people as revealed by (1) regularity of attendance, (2) punctuality, (3) concentration of attention, (4) co-operation with ushers, (6) courtesy toward visitors, (7) appreciation of leadership, (8) prayerful concern for results, (9) interest in total church program, (10) orderliness with friendliness on dismissal.

A service of corporate worship is a co-operative enterprise. Studies may well be made as to the degree with which the several parts and movements have been integrated. Such a check will concentrate attention on (1) the caretaker's part in preparing the place of worship; (2) the ushers' part in preventing distractions; (3) the congregation's part, as guided by an attractive bulletin; (4) the minister's part in fitting Scripture reading, prayer, and sermon into the total pattern; (6) the chorister's part in relating the music to the minister's purpose; (7) the organist or pianist's part in skilful accompaniment and choice of appropriate selections; (8) the choir's part in effective leadership of congregational singing and in the rendering of choral selections; (9) the deacons' part as they exercise supervisory care over the total service; (10) the Holy Spirit's part as his promised guidance is sought and followed.

Objective evaluation of worship should be matched by subjective evaluation. Even more important are the outcomes of worship in terms of changes in the lives of persons.

Worship should result in changed attitudes. Jesus emphasized inward motives more than he did outward conduct. He knew that murder is preceded by hatred, that adultery arises from impure desire. Prior to evil speech are evil attitudes, "for out of the abundance of the heart the mouth speaks" (Matt. 12:34). More important than the act of worship is the right or wrong attitude which one has toward his brother: "So if you are offering your gift at the altar, and there remember that your brother has something against you, leave your gift there before the altar and go; first be reconciled to your brother, and then come and offer your gift" (Matt. 5: 23-24).

It would be illuminating if not terrifying if the minister, standing before his congregation, could penetrate beneath decorous exteriors. He would no doubt observe attitudes of indifference, cynicism, suspicion, prejudice, superiority, inferiority, self-pity, resentment. Lecturing, moralizing, censuring, and condemning usually do little to bring about the needed change; only the transforming power of an experience of worship will suffice.

The emotions are of vast importance for human living. Attitudes indicate the direction in which life moves; emotions propel toward the goal.

Again, it would be startling if the minister and his associates could look into the impassive faces of the congregation and see underneath the feelings that stir them. Many of these feelings are hurtful to the point of being destructive—anger, malice, unforgiveness, wounded pride, perverted ambition, impure desire, self-centeredness, covetousness, retaliation, fear, anxiety, pessimism, and similar emotions that move life in the wrong direction.

Worship can turn emotions into helpful channels. In a meaningful confrontation with God, anger can be changed into kindness; malice into goodwill; unforgiveness into forgiveness; wounded pride into reconciliation; perverted ambition into holy aspiration; impure desire into purity of heart; self-centeredness into philanthropy; covetousness into generosity; fear into courage; anxiety into peace of mind; retaliation into gentleness; pessimism into optimism. Such results are often by-products of a worship experience. If there are no such results, worship services come under judgment.

Attitudes and emotions are preparatory to action. If action is blocked or misdirected, damage is done. Much derangement of personality is due to the overstimulation in today's culture that does not find healthy response in action. Worship services may inadvertently contribute to this damage. Attitudes may be formed, feelings may be aroused, the congregation may then be dismissed with a feeling of futility. A service of worship should therefore be evaluated in terms of conduct responses.

Has the experience of worship helped the participants to behave more kindly, more generously, more honestly, more truthfully, more sincerely, more law-abidingly, more courageously, more self-sacrificingly, more usefully in their interpersonal relationships, and in their civic, social, and occupational responsibilities? The question is not easily answered, for there are many interrelated factors, but conscientious leaders of worship should look for evidence of changes in individual conduct attributable to the worship services.

Much of life is controlled by habit patterns. Some habits are acquired unreflectively; others are due to thoughtful choices. Worship may be evaluated in terms of choices that lead to habits. The habit of church attendance may have in it some element of the automatic but in the main it is a habit formed and maintained by choice.

The experience of worship is a determiner of choice. "Choose you this day" is the expressed or implied exhortation involved in every worship service. There are choices of regular attendance, of systematic and worthy giving, of sustained Bible reading and prayer, of witnessing to the unsaved, of serving those in need, of befriending the friendless, of refusing to take unfair advantage, of yielding self-will to the will of God. There are innumerable daily choices between self-interest and the welfare of others. These choices need a con-trolling center so that each choice does not have to be reviewed each time but decision is made according to established principles. Worship puts God at the center and establishes as the principle the example of Christ. How effective is worship in achieving this out-come? The answer may not be given statistically, but if worship is vital an affirmative answer should be evident as the lives of wor-shipers are observed.

Destiny hangs on the outcomes of worship. Are unbelievers con-fronted with Christ and his claims so persuasively that they accept him as Saviour and Lord? Are lives so remade that they withstand the temptations of the world, the flesh, the devil? Are families so bound together that they resist the forces of disorganization? Are young people sent out into the world with strength of character to make their lives count for Christ? Are men and women dismissed from the worship services to go into politics, business, industry, the professions and occupations, having put on the whole armor of God that they may be able to withstand the evil day, and having done all, to stand? Can it be truthfully said of those who participate in the services of worship that they are the salt of the earth, the light of the world?

These are searching questions to be answered faithfully by those responsible for services of worship and by these answers worship is to be evaluated. Jesus himself proposed the test: "You will know them by their fruits. Are grapes gathered from thorns, or figs from thistles? So, every sound tree bears good fruit, but the bad tree bears evil fruit. . . . Every tree that does not bear good fruit is cut down and thrown into the fire. Thus you will know them by their fruits" (Matt. 7:16-20). Perhaps to nothing could these words be more aptly applied than to a church and its worship.

Worship may be evaluated with reference to certain basic guiding principles. It may be assumed that an activity is more valuable if it accords with fundamental truth from which procedures are de-rived—a core about which particulars are gathered. Activities which constitute the worship service may be marked by two contrasting faults—overemphasis on theology, or overemphasis on methodology. In the first instance, the minister is absorbed in his message to which other aspects of the service are incidental. Accordingly, principles of worship are ignored and procedures may be haphazard or stereotyped. In the opposite situation, major concern is for an attractive service, with tuneful singing, variety of special features, maximum congregational participation, unusual and entertaining preaching— all designed to attract and hold an audience. Here too the ideal of worship may be obscured from lack of guiding principles. Both the "egghead" and the "vaudeville" types of churches need the corrective of critical examination of their patterns of worship in the light of normative principles.

Worship may be tested by the principles of readiness. It is axiomatic that worship is facilitated when there is readiness to worship. Obviously this principle is violated when there is lack of preparation on the part of leaders of worship, when there is confusion or disorder before the beginning of worship, or when there is no apparent consciousness on the part of those present that they have assembled for worship. The principle of readiness is observed when leaders are well prepared and when the people, conscious of the presence of God, assemble with reverent quietness and the intention of worshiping. *Measured by this principle, how would a given worship service rate?*

Worship may be tested by the principle of unity. There is need of a total pattern into which the several parts fit naturally and appropriately. This does not imply a stereotyped order with dull regularity; the pattern is made more attractive when there is suitable variety. Yet if the parts lack relatedness, with no controlling *motif*, the impression is that of fragmentation with resultant incoherent experience. The principle is violated when the songs are selected at random, the instrumental music takes no account of mood and purpose of the sermon, the Scripture reading and prayers are irrelevant to the objectives of the sermon, the congregation's thoughts are scattered and attention lacks concentration. *Measured by this principle, how does a given worship service rate?*

Worship may be tested by the principle of movement. A church may repeat its order of services with such deadly regularity and uniformity that the breath of life goes from it. There may be merely a succession of formalized acts, much as when bricks are laid; the result is an inanimate structure rather than a living organism. The New Testament represents the church as the body of Christ, not just an organization but an organism, by means of which he carries out his purposes in the world. A church at worship is a church getting its instruction and inspiration to fulfil its function as Christ's living body. Dullness, lethargy, static, automation, lack of movement, are inexcusable in the worship of a church that claims identity with its living Lord. *Tested by this principle, how does a given worship service rate?*

Worship may be tested by the principle of economy. "The hour of worship" is taken quite literally in today's world. None of the golden sixty minutes of the hour should be wasted. The movement of worship should be unhurried, yet the service should begin on time and close on time. Whatever is unnecessary or irrelevant should be eliminated. Those who guide radio and television programs know that they are under the control of the minute and even the second hand of the clock. Those who lead worship are not under such inexorable requirement but they should no less carefully conserve the time of the congregation. Each part of the service may be scheduled so that it will have its proper place without encroachment on some other part and without unduly continuing the service beyond the appointed time of dismissal. To the service of this meaningful hour should be brought all the spiritual resources of leaders and congregation to the end that nothing be wasted. *Tested by this principle, how does a given worship service rate?*

Worship may be tested by the principle of dignity. There is something essentially incongruous about an undignified service of worship. Dignity does not imply stiffness, formality, unnaturalness, aloofness. True dignity connotes innate merit, worth, genuineness. A service of worship to be dignified does not have to be gloomy, forbidding, austere, inhuman. This sort of false dignity Jesus condemned, as in the case of the hypocritical Pharisees who offered long prayers and disfigured their faces "to be seen by men"; rather, he approved simplicity and naturalness in prayer and worship, with heads anointed and faces washed and with radiant and joyous spirits. His example of seriousness and gravity and the very nature of worship itself would preclude triviality and all buffoonery. *Tested by this principle of dignity, how would a given worship service rate?*

Worship may be tested by the principle of beauty. Beauty is an indefinable but very real quality. God's holiness should never be dissociated from his beauty. There is an inseparable relation between beauty and goodness, ugliness and evil. All that men call beautiful may not be good and all that men adjudge ugly may not be bad, but whatever is holy is beautiful and whatever is evil is ugly. Ugliness in worship is intuitively repulsive. No matter what its outward appearance, a house of worship may be made beautiful by the tender, loving care of its members. No matter how barren of aesthetic adornment, a service of worship may be made beautiful by the reverent spirit of leaders and congregation. Walls may be kept painted, windows may be cleaned, the interior of the sanctuary may be immaculate, the hymnbooks may be neatly bound, the atmosphere may be that of reverence. To the worshiper, the place and the service of worship should always be beautiful. *Tested by this principle, how does a given worship service rate?*

Worship may be tested by the principle of mystery. God is spirit but we who worship him must worship with spirits encased in flesh. God does not live in shrines made by man but we need a place to worship that has been built by hands. Always there is an element of mystery when the human seeks communion with the divine. In an experience of worship, there is more than human response to a material situation of stimulation: "For heaven comes down our souls to greet, and glory crowns the mercy seat."

Never to be lost is this sense of awe in the presence of the *mysterium tremendum*. Always to be shunned is overfamiliarity with God and the things of God. This principle is violated when the music partakes too much of the spirit of the world, when the poetry of the songs is too light and sentimental, when the prayers are addressed to the congregation rather than to God, when the leaders of

worship are too jocular or frivolous, when the sermon is secular
rather than spiritual. Jesus taught us to say, "Our Father," but he
also taught us to say, "Hallowed be thy name." *Tested by this principle of mystery, how would a given worship service rate?*

Worship may be tested by the principle of democracy. At the
heart of true democracy is respect for personality, and respect for
persons should characterize Christian worship. Worship fulfils its
purpose best when every person present feels wanted and included.
Worship suffers serious loss when members of the congregation do
not participate because their interests and needs and capacities have
not been considered. Leaders lead best when their leadership is all
but unnoticed as the whole congregation accepts responsibility and
takes initiative. Worship is hindered in its expression of democracy
when leaders become too prominent and the people too dependent.
It is in such democratic togetherness of worship that Christians
achieve "power to comprehend with all the saints what is the
breadth and length and height and depth, and to know the love of
Christ which surpasses knowledge" (Eph. 3:18-19). *Tested by
this democratic principle, how would a given worship service rate?*

Worship may be tested by the principle of reality. Dean Sperry
considered this the ultimate test. He wrote:

Is what we have now before us real? Is it true in itself? Is it true
for us? Is there anything in our own lives as Christians to which it
corresponds, and which it helps us to say out, simply and directly to
God and to each other? If it is thus real, well and good. It stands
approved. If it does not ring true, what is the trouble? Is it patently
insincere, symbolizing or saying something which we do not believe?
Then it must go. If we are not conscious of actual inconsistency and
insincerity, but only of a half-alive truthfulness, again what is the
matter? Are we only half in earnest religiously, or is this symbol or
custom inadequate and incapable today of witnessing to truth? If the
trouble is with us, how shall we set about remedying it? If the trouble
is with this bit of church furniture or liturgy, can we find a better
medium for the expression of our Christianity? If we would once subject the whole apparatus of worship to some such tests as these we
should begin to get some light on the causes of the unreality and in-
effectualness of much of our worship.[1]

McNutt translated reality into terms of relevancy: "Worship must keep the feet of the worshiper on the ground and forbid his blinking at any of the facts of his earthly existence. Worship should aim to open the doors and windows of his whole being to the Divine so that thus re-empowered and suffused with a more than human strength he may overcome his own world and finally receive the victor's crown and his Master's 'Well done, good and faithful servant.' "[2]

Worship may be tested by the principle of purpose. Worship is not passive but purposive. It is communion with God in seeking to discover and to do his will. Worship calls on the worshiper to do his part and to do his best. Intention will not suffice for action; thought will not substitute for deed; saying "Amen" will not replace saying "I will."

Worship is not a spectator activity. True worshipers are not on the sidelines, they are not even the cheerleaders—they are the players in the game. There are souls to be saved; there are churches to be built; there are missionaries to be sent and supported; there are great causes to be espoused; there are evils to be banished and the kingdom of God to be enlarged; there are battles to be fought against the forces of wrong with a world at stake. Worship equips us with undefeatable purpose for the conquest in the realization that "we are not contending against flesh and blood, but against the principalities, against the powers, against the world rulers of this present darkness, against the spiritual hosts of wickedness in the heavenly places" (Eph. 6:12). Purposeless worship is powerless worship.

The growing of a church that seeks continuously to measure up to these high ideals is the supreme achievement of Christians who accept their commission as workers together with God in carrying out the purposes of Jesus Christ. This is the church at worship.

Notes

Chapter 1

1. The *San Francisco Chronicle*, August 26, 1960.

Chapter 3

1. William D. Maxwell, *An Outline of Christian Worship* (London: Oxford University Press, 1936), p. 17.

Chapter 4

1. J. Robert Nelson, *The Realm of Redemption,* (Greenwich, Connecticut: Seabury Press).

2. John Dewey, *Democracy and Education* (New York: The Macmillan Co., 1916).

3. Bertrand Russell, *Why Men Fight* (New York: Appleton-Century Crofts, 1917).

Chapter 5

1. Charles H. Heimsath, *The Genius of Public Worship* (New York: Charles Scribner's Sons, 1944), p. 47.

2. D. H. Hislop, *Our Heritage in Public Worship* (Edinburgh: T. & T. Clark), p. 93.

3. *Ibid.,* p. 95.

4. *Ibid.,* pp. 95-96.

5. *Ibid.,* p. 99.

6. *Ibid.,* p. 100.

7. *Ibid.*

8. *Ibid.,* p. 101.

9. *Ibid.*

10. *Ibid.,* p. 133.

11. *Ibid.,* pp. 131-32.

12. *Ibid.,* p. 129.

13. Austin C. Lovelace and William C. Rice, *Music and Worship in the Church* (New York: Abingdon Press, 1960), Glossary, p. 196.

14. Hislop, *op. cit.,* p. 200.

Chapter 6

1. Scott Francis Brenner, *The Way of Worship* (New York: The Macmillan Co., 1944), p. 128.

2. John Henry Jowett, *The Preacher, His Life and Work* (New

York: Formerly published by Doubleday; used by permission of Harper & Brothers, 1912), pp. 45-46.

3. Henry Sloane Coffin, *The Public Worship of God* (Philadelphia: The Westminster Press, Copyright 1946, W. L. Jenkins), pp. 70-96. Used by permission.

4. Norman Cousins, "Ministerial Corn," *Saturday Review* (New York: Saturday Review, Inc., November 23, 1946. [These comments are put in the words of a fictitious farmer and are not a direct quote from Norman Cousins]), p. 22.

Chapter 7

1. Arthur Elson, *The Book of Musical Knowledge* (New York: Tudor Publishing Co., 1927), p. 3.

2. Winfred Douglas, *Church Music in History and Practice* (New York: Charles Scribner's Sons, 1937), p. 13.

3. Quoted by Erik Routley, *The Church and Music* (London: Gerald Duckworth & Co., Ltd., 1950), p. 121.

4. Percy Scholes, *The Puritans and Music in England and New England* (London: Oxford University Press, 1934).

5. Edward Dickinson, *Music in the History of the Western Church* (New York: Charles Scribner's Sons, 1902), p. 316.

6. Bernard L. Manning, *The Hymns of Wesley and Watts* (London: The Epworth Press, 1942), p. 14.

7. Oliver Strunk, *Source Readings in Music History* (New York: W. W. Norton & Co., 1950), I, 65.

8. Dickinson, *op. cit.,* p. 397.

Chapter 8

1. Brenner, *op. cit.,* p. 137.

2. William Roy McNutt, *Worship in the Churches* (Philadelphia: Judson Press, 1941), p. 117. Used by permission.

3. Albert W. Palmer, *The Art of Conducting Public Worship* (New York: The Macmillan Co., 1939), p. 12.

4. Carroll A. Wise, *Religion in Illness and Health* (New York: Harper & Brothers, 1942), pp. 141-42.

5. See James Dalton Morrison (ed.), *Masterpieces of Religious Verse* (New York: Harper & Brothers, 1948). Used by permission C. Wallis.

6. Fred Eastman and Louis Wilson, *Drama in the Church* (Copyright, 1933, by Samuel French. Copyright, 1960 (in renewal), by Fred Eastman. All rights reserved. Reprinted by permission of the authors and Samuel French, Inc., pp. 17-18.

Chapter 9

1. Bernard C. Clausen, *The Technique of a Minister* (New York: Fleming H. Revell Co., 1925), p. 111.

2. George A. Buttrick, *Prayer* (New York: Abingdon Press, 1953). (The quotation at the end of the excerpt reading "Prayer is the very sword of the Saints" is quoted from Francis Thompson, *Health and Holiness,* p. 16.)

3. Pamphlet, "Yokefellow Associates," 1908 Grand Avenue, Nashville, Tennessee. See also Elton Trueblood, *A Manual for Prayer Groups,* 1908 Grand Avenue, Nashville, Tennessee.

Chapter 10

1. E. D. Starbuck, *The Psychology of Religion* (New York: Charles Scribner's Sons, 1899).

2. William James, *The Varieties of Religious Experience* (New York: Longmans, Green & Co., 1902).

3. Wayne E. Oates, *Religious Factors in Mental Illness* (New York: Association Press, 1955), p. 147.

4. Russell J. Becker, "Links Between Psychology and Religion," *Pastoral Psychology* (May, 1961), p. 13. Reprinted by permission Pastoral Psychology Press.

Chapter 12

1. Willard L. Sperry, *Reality in Worship* (New York: The Macmillan Co., 1925), pp: 211-12.

2. McNutt, *op. cit.,* p. 59.

For Further Reading

ANGYAL, ANDRAS. *Foundation for a Science of Personality*. New York: The Commonwealth Fund, 1941.

ASHTON, JOSEPH N. *Music in Worship*. Boston: The Pilgrim Press, 1944.

BAILLIE, JOHN. *A Diary of Private Prayer*. New York: Charles Scribner's Sons, 1949.

BAKER, EDNA DEAN. *The Worship of the Little Child*. Nashville: Cokesbury Press, 1927.

BALDWIN, JOSEPH L. *Worship Training for Juniors*. New York: The Methodist Book Concern, 1927.

BARLOW, WALTER. *God So Loved*. Westwood, New Jersey: Fleming H. Revell Co., 1952.

BARRETT, ALBERT M. *People Under Pressure*. New York: Twayne Publishers, Inc., 1960.

BAUER, MARION. *Twentieth-Century Music*. New York: G. P. Putnam's Sons, 1947.

BAYS, ALICE A. *Worship Services for Purposeful Living*. New York: Abingdon Press, 1949.

BLACKWOOD, ANDREW W. *Evangelism in the Home Church*. New York: Abingdon Press, 1942.

———. *The Fine Art of Public Worship*. New York: Abingdon-Cokesbury Press, 1939.

BRENNER, SCOTT F. *The Way of Worship*. New York: The Macmillan Co., 1944.

BROWN, HELEN ADA, and HELTMAN, H. J. (eds.). *Choral Readings for Worship and Inspiration*. Philadelphia: The Westminster Press, 1954.

BUTTRICK, GEORGE A. *Prayer*. New York: Abingdon Press, 1942.

BYINGTON, EDWIN H. *The Quest for Experience in Worship*. New York: Harper & Brothers, 1929.

CASTEEL, JOHN. *Spiritual Renewal Through Personal Groups*. New York: Association Press, 1957.

COFFIN, HENRY S. *The Public Worship of God*. Philadelphia: The Westminster Press, 1946.

CULLMAN, OSCAR. *Early Christian Worship*. Translated by A. STEWART TODD and JAMES B. TORRANCE. London: SCM Press, 1953.

CURTIS, ELNORA W. *The Dramatic Instinct in Education*. Boston: Houghton Mifflin Co., 1914.

DAVIES, HENRY W. *Music and Worship*. London: Eyre & Spottiswoode, 1948.

DAVIES, HORTON. *Christian Worship: Its History and Meaning*. New York: Abingdon Press, 1957.

DOBBINS, GAINES S. *Evangelism According to Christ*. Nashville, Tennessee: Broadman Press, 1949.

———, *Winning the Children*. Nashville: Broadman Press, 1953.

DOBSON, J. O. *Worship*. London: Student Christian Movement Press, 1941.

DUCHESNE, LOUIS M. *Christian Worship: Its Origin and Evolution*. London: Society for Promoting Christian Knowledge, 1954.

EWEN, DAVID. *Music Comes to America* (rev. ed.). New York: Allen, Towne & Heath, 1947.

FERM, R. O. *The Psychology of Christian Conversion*. Westwood, New Jersey: Fleming H. Revell Co., 1959.

GAGE, ALBERT H. *Increasing Church Attendance*. Grand Rapids, Michigan: Zondervan Publishing House, 1953.

GREENE, EDWARD B. *Measurements of Human Behavior* (rev. ed.). New York: The Odyssey Press, 1952.

HARDMAN, OSCAR. *A History of Christian Worship*. Nashville: Cokesbury Press, 1937.

HAZELTON, ROGER. *The God We Worship*. New York: The Macmillan Company, 1946.

HEBERT, A. G. *Liturgy and Society*. London: Faber & Faber, Ltd., 1935.

HEDLEY, GEORGE. *Christian Worship*. New York: The Macmillan Co., 1953.

HENRY, NELSON B. (ed.). *Forty-fifth Yearbook, The Measurement of Understanding*. Chicago: The University of Chicago Press, 1946.

HILTNER, SEWARD. *Pastoral Counseling*. New York: Abingdon Press, 1949.

———. *Self-Understanding Through Psychology and Religion*. New York: Charles Scribner's Sons, 1951.

HISLOP, DAVID H. *Our Heritage in Public Worship*. Edinburgh: T. & T. Clark, 1935.

HORTON, DOUGLAS. *The Meaning of Worship*. New York: Harper & Brothers, 1959.

HUNTER, STANLEY A. *Music and Religion*. New York: Abingdon Press, 1930.

HUSS, JOHN. *The Hour of Power*. Grand Rapids, Michigan: Zondervan Publishing House, 1945.

HUXTABLE, JOHN, et al. *A Book of Public Worship*. London: Oxford University Press, 1949.

JACKAWAY, CLARICE M. *The Tapestry of Life*. New York: The Exposition Press, Inc., 1955.

JOHNSON, PAUL E. *Psychology of Pastoral Care*. New York: Abingdon Press, 1953.

———. *Psychology of Religion* (rev. ed.). New York: Abingdon Press, 1959.

JONES, ILION T. *A Historical Approach to Evangelical Worship*. New York: Abingdon Press, 1954.

KENNEDY, JOHN. *The God Whom We Ignore*. New York: The Macmillan Co., 1938.

KERR, P. S. *Music in Evangelism, and Stories of Famous Christian Songs*. Glendale, California: Gospel Music Publishers, 1944.

KOHLER, WOLFGANG. *The Place of Value in a World of Facts*. New York: Liveright Publishing Corp., 1938.

LEE, ROY STUART. *Psychology and Worship*. London: SCM Press, 1955.

LLOYD, L. S. *Music and Sound*. London: Oxford University Press, 1951.

LOVELACE, AUSTIN C., and RICE, WILLIAM C. *Music and Worship in the Church*. New York: Abingdon Press, 1960.

MACDONALD, ALEXANDER B. *Christian Worship in the Primitive Church*. Edinburgh: T. & T. Clark, 1934.

McDORMAND, THOMAS B. *The Art of Building Worship Services*. (rev. ed.). Nashville: Broadman Press, 1958.

McKINNEY, HOWARD D., and ANDERSON, W. R. *Discovering Music*. New York: American Book Co., 1952.

McNUTT, WILLIAM R. *Worship in the Churches*. Philadelphia: The Judson Press, 1941.

MARTIN, A. W. *Worship in the Sunday School for Workers in Small Schools*. New York: Abingdon Press, 1943.

MELAND, BERNARD E. *Seeds of Redemption*. New York: The Macmillan Company, 1947.

MUNRO, HARRY C. *Fellowship Evangelism Through Church Groups*. St. Louis: Bethany Press, 1951.

MYERS, A. J. WILLIAM (ed.). *Enriching Worship*. New York: Harper & Brothers, 1949.

NILES, DANIEL T. *That They May Have Life*. New York: Harper and Brothers, 1951.

OATES, WAYNE E. *Religious Factors in Mental Illness*. New York: Association Press, 1955.

———. *The Bible in Pastoral Care*. Philadelphia: The Westminster Press, 1953.

PALMER, ALBERT W. *The Art of Conducting Public Worship*. New York: The Macmillan Co., 1939.

PALMER, GORDON. *Manual of Church Services*. Westwood, N. J.: Fleming H. Revell Co., 1947.

PARROTT, LORA L. *Devotional Programs for Women's Groups.* Grand Rapids, Michigan: Zondervan Publishing House, 1952.

PAST, MARY E. *Intermediates' Worship Programs.* Westwood, N. J.: Fleming H. Revell Co., 1942.

PHILLIPS, JOHN B. *Appointment with God.* New York: The Macmillan Company, 1954.

PLEUTHNER, WILLARD A. *Building Up Your Congregation.* New York: Wilcox & Follett Co., 1951.

PORTER, DAVID R. (ed.). *Worship Resources for Youth.* New York: Association Press, 1948.

POWELL, MARIE COLE. *Boys and Girls at Worship.* New York: Harper & Brothers, 1943.

POWELL, SIDNEY W. *Where Are the People?* New York: Abingdon Press, 1953.

REYNOLDS, I. E. *Music and the Scriptures.* Nashville: Broadman Press, 1942.

ROUTLEY, ERIK. *The Church and Music.* London: Gerald Duckworth & Co., Ltd., 1950.

SANGSTER, WILLIAM E. *Let Me Commend.* New York: Abingdon Press, 1948.

SWEAZEY, GEORGE E. *Effective Evangelism.* New York: Harper & Brothers, 1953.

TOMPKINS, OLIVER S. (ed.). *World Conference on Faith and Order.* London: SCM Press, 1953.

TOURNIER, PAUL. *The Meaning of Persons.* New York: Harper & Brothers, 1957.

TRUEBLOOD, DAVID E. *Confronting Christ.* New York: Harper & Brothers, 1960.

UNDERHILL, EVELYN. *Worship.* New York: Harper & Brothers, 1937.

VOGT, VON OGDEN. *Art and Religion.* New Haven, Connecticut: Yale University Press, 1921.

VERKUYL, GERRIT. *Teen-age Worship.* Chicago: Moody Press, 1950.

WALLIS, CHARLES L. *Worship Resources for the Christian Year.* New York: Harper & Brothers, 1954.

WEISER, THERESA. *Music for God.* New York: Philosophical Library, 1951.

WHITE, ROBERT W. *Lives in Progress.* New York: The Dryden Press, Inc., 1952.

WISE, CARROLL A. *Religion in Illness and Health.* New York: Harper & Brothers, 1942.

WYGAL, WINNIFRED. *How to Plan Informal Worship.* New York: Association Press, 1955.

————. *Reflections of the Spirit.* New York: Woman's Press, 1948.

Index

DATE DUE

6-13-06		
7-20-06		
12-2-08		